T5-AFF-934

Dover Opera Guide and Libretto Series

LA BOHÈME

By

GIACOMO PUCCINI

Translated and Introduced

By

ELLEN H. BLEILER

DOVER PUBLICATIONS, INC.

New York

Published simultaneously in Canada by McClelland and Stewart Ltd.

Published in the United Kingdom by Constable and Company Limited, 10 Orange Street, London W.C.2.

This new Dover edition, first published in 1962, contains the following material:

The standard authorized Italian libretto of *La Bohème*, as originally published by G. Ricordi & Company in 1896.

A new English translation of the libretto and supplementary material by Ellen H. Bleiler.

Illustrations for this edition have been selected from various sources.

Manufactured in the United States of America

Dover Publications, Inc.
180 Varick Street
New York 14, N.Y.

CONTENTS

THE COMPOSER

Lucca is a medium-sized Italian city northeast of Pisa, in the fertile valley of the Serchio River. The people of the area farm the rich Tuscan soil; for centuries the town itself has contributed to northern Italy's silk industry. To Lucca, early in the eighteenth century, came the Puccinis. For almost 150 years they occupied honored places there as composers of sacred and secular music, leaders of church choirs, and cathedral organists.

Giacomo Puccini belonged to the fifth generation of this rather illustrious family. Michele, his father, had studied in Bologna. Michele's quest for musical knowledge carried him as far as Naples, where he worked for a time under Donizetti. Upon returning to Lucca, Michele Puccini taught both privately and at the local music school, the Pacini Institute; he also followed family tradition by playing the cathedral organ and composing religious music, which won him considerable renown in the area. Michele Puccini died in 1863, leaving a thirty-three-year-old wife, Albina Magi Puccini, with the care of six young children and one soon to be born. Giacomo, born on December 22 or 23, 1858, was the fifth of these children; he had one brother and five sisters.

Less than six years old when his father died, Giacomo could recall one aspect of his earliest musical training. His father had placed coins on certain organ keys as an incentive to Giacomo to press those notes, since the boy was still much too small to read music.

Albina Puccini could give her children the necessities of life, but little else. Naturally, she expected that Giacomo, the elder son, would follow the family profession. Lucca reserved the posts of cathedral organist and choirmaster for Giacomo at such time as he had knowledge and ability to occupy them.

Despite his mother's hopes for him, it seemed doubtful that young Giacomo would ever have sufficient training, not to mention energy, to fill the positions held by so many of his respected forebears. He did rather poorly at school; sent to the Pacini Institute to be taught music by his uncle Fortunato Magi, he showed neither much musical interest nor inclination to study. He was a moody boy whose chief pleasures seem to have been hunting birds and, from quite an early age, smoking cigarettes. Magi complained to his sister that her son lacked talent and had no business attending a music school. Somewhat despairingly, Puccini's mother begged another of the Institute's teachers to see what he could do with Giacomo. Fortunately, this man understood young Puccini much better than did his predecessor; he was patient with the boy and presently managed to develop Puccini's innate musical talent. Puccini decided to become a musician after all. He managed to contribute to his family's meager income by giving piano and organ lessons. It looked as if yet another Puccini would soon place his name in Lucca's musical annals.

To the age of eighteen, Giacomo had apparently never seen an opera, although he had heard his teacher describe several. One opera of which the teacher spoke was Verdi's recent renowned success, *Aida*. When Puccini heard that a performance of *Aida* was scheduled for Pisa's opera house, he determined to attend, although he could certainly not afford even the train fare between Lucca and Pisa. Undaunted, he set out on foot early on the day of the opera, and returned by the same method late that night—a distance of almost twenty miles each way! It must have been quite a performance; according to friends and biographers of Puccini, it was this experience which made the boy resolve then and there to become a composer of operas.

To realize this ambition, Puccini knew he needed more musical training than he could have in Lucca. Somehow he must be admitted to the Royal Conservatory of Music in Milan—that pinnacle of Italian opera. Puccini was fully aware that his mother could not possibly afford to send him to the Conservatory—to go there he would have to win a scholarship. But scholarship applicants had to be able to claim a certain amount of actual achievement. Hopefully, Puccini entered a musical competition which Lucca was holding; he lost resoundingly. The next year he tried again—this time with a motet written for the feast of the town's patron saint—and won. Through influential friends of his mother, he managed to get a scholarship for one year to the Milan Conservatory from Queen Margherita; and in the fall of 1880, full of high hopes and expectations, Puccini left for Milan.

Like most young people who come from provincial towns to a large, bustling metropolis, Puccini was awed by Milan. Its size, commerce, and wealth fascinated him, although in later life he grew to dislike the city. Some of Italy's leading composers taught at the Royal Conservatory. Among these famous men, one who took a special interest in the student from Lucca was Amilcare Ponchielli. Today Ponchielli is remembered primarily as the composer of that rather astonishing opera *La Gioconda*; in his own time however, his other works were acclaimed too, and Puccini was indeed lucky to become a protégé of this kindly gentleman.

During his second and third years at the Conservatory, Puccini was no longer aided by the Queen's scholarship. Although both his mother and a Lucca relative managed to contribute a little to his support, Puccini learned the meaning of real poverty in those days. In a famous and often-quoted letter to his mother, he begged for a tiny amount of olive oil—apparently an unobtainable delicacy in Milan—in order to cook beans for himself as he liked them. Still, he managed to see as many opera performances as he could, borrowing the money for tickets, or even talking his way into performances. Their fascination for him constantly increased, and he apparently never wavered in his ambition to become an operatic composer.

Presently, Puccini was joined in his small room by his younger brother Michele, who was also a music student, and then by a poor cousin. Much later, Puccini told how the three students had been strictly forbidden by their landlord to cook in their room. But dining out was too expensive; and so the other two boys would be chefs, while Puccini pounded on the piano as loudly as he could to drown out their culinary noises. Puccini's feelings about landlords, he himself admitted, carried over into *La Bohème*. Toward the end of his stay at the Conservatory, Puccini roomed with another student, a boy who, though several years his junior, already had a good deal of practical experience as a musician. This boy would also be famous one day: his name was Pietro Mascagni, and he composed an opera named *Cavalleria Rusticana.*

Before they could be graduated from the Conservatory with the title of "Maestro," all students had to submit to the faculty an original composition which would be performed at a student concert attended by some leading music critics. Puccini's composition for this event was a "Capriccio Sinfonico." (It remains one of his few known non-operatic works.) The "Capriccio" was favorably received; it was praised even by the eminent critic Filippi,* published by the firm of Lucca, and displayed in music store windows. And so, in July 1863, with the pleasant sounds of success still in his ears, Maestro Giacomo Puccini prepared to embark upon the next phase of his career.

Puccini returned to Lucca somewhat at loose ends. He was more certain than ever of wanting to compose an opera. But operas need libretti, and libretti are seldom written as acts of charity for unknown and penniless young composers. Seldom—but not quite never. At any rate, if Puccini's first libretto was not presented to him exactly as an act of charity, it at least owed its existence directly to the kindness and persuasiveness of his former teacher, Ponchielli. The latter knew a young poet, Ferdinando Fontana, and persuaded this man to write a short libretto for the recent Conservatory graduate, in whose talent Ponchielli seemed to have genuine faith, and about whose inability to pay for the work he was perfectly frank with Fontana.

The result of Puccini's first collaboration was a short opera, *Le Villi.* It concerns tragic death and vengeful spooks in the Black Forest (leaving little doubt that librettist and composer, like so many of their contemporaries, had succumbed to the current German influence). Puccini entered *Le Villi* in a prize contest; once again he lost, and the whole project would have ended there, had not Fontana come to the rescue. The poet persuaded some influential friends, among them the composer-librettist Arrigo Boito, to take an interest in *Le Villi.* Backing was obtained, and money to produce the opera was raised. *Le Villi* was performed in May 1884 at Milan's Teatro dal Verme. Now forgotten, it was enthusiastically received by both critics and audience. As a result, Puccini found his financial credit greatly improved; but undoubtedly the

* Best known for his trip to Egypt to attend the première of *Aida.*

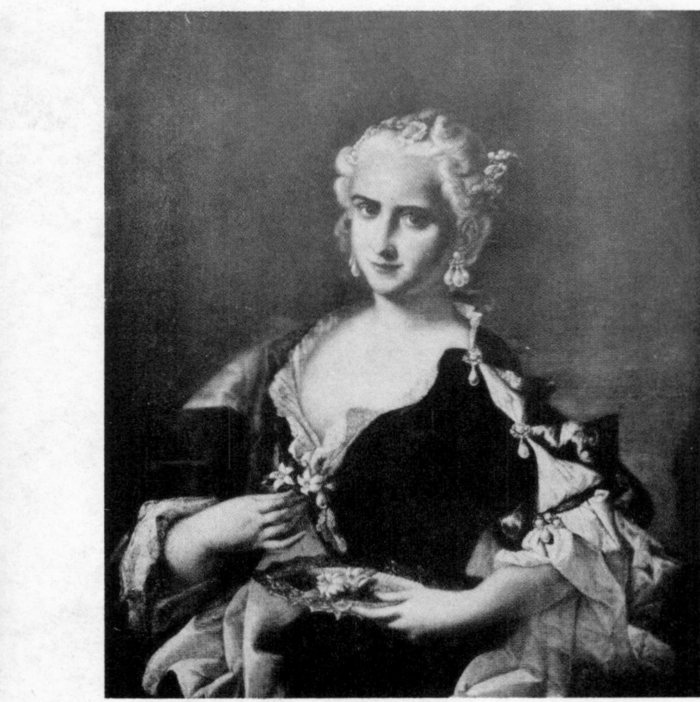

(Marchetti, Leopoldo: *Puccini nelle Immagini*. Published by Garzanti, Milan, 1949)   (Courtesy Rita Puccini)

The first Giacomo Puccini, born in Lucca in 1712 and buried in the cathedral there.

Wife of the first Giacomo Puccini.

(Puccini nelle Immagini)

The house where Puccini was born, Via del Poggio, Lucca.

(*Puccini nelle Immagini,* courtesy Rita Puccini)

Michele Puccini, Giacomo's father, a composer in his own right.

Albina Magi Puccini, Giacomo's mother.

(*Puccini nelle Immagini,* courtesy Rita Puccini)

Giacomo Puccini as a student in Lucca.

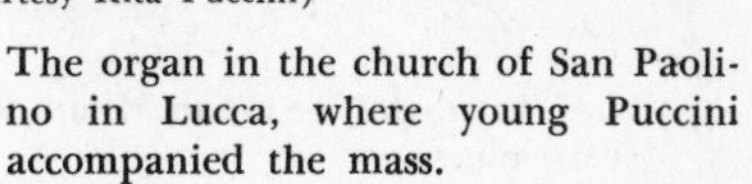

The organ in the church of San Paolino in Lucca, where young Puccini accompanied the mass.

(*Puccini nelle Immagini*)

The Royal Conservatory of Music in Milan.

(*Puccini nelle Immagini*)

The Teatro Dal Verme in Milan, where Puccini's first opera, *Le Villi,* received its première.

most important effect of *Le Villi's* success was that it further developed his life-long association with Giulio Ricordi, head of Europe's most important music-publishing firm; mentor, counsel, and sponsor to some of the world's greatest composers. Ricordi bought the rights to *Le Villi* and commissioned Puccini to write another opera—this one to receive its première at La Scala.

Edgar, Puccini's second opera, was again the result of a collaboration with Ferdinando Fontana. It was completed in 1888 and performed in April 1889. Unlike some of his illustrious predecessors—Donizetti or Rossini, for instance—who could cheerfully produce an opera in a couple of weeks,* Puccini usually spent three or four years on each of his works. During his early years as a composer, he literally owed his livelihood between premières to the generosity and confidence (both later amply rewarded) of Giulio Ricordi. *Edgar* got a lukewarm reception; during its composer's lifetime it was occasionally performed; after his death in 1924, it supplied his funeral elegy, conducted by Toscanini in the Milan Cathedral. Now it has sunk into operatic oblivion.

Perhaps because several critics blamed *Edgar's* failure on its foolish libretto, Puccini, from then on, became one of opera's hardest to please and most exacting taskmasters where libretti were concerned. Perhaps he finally acknowledged to himself—as he openly stated later—that his greatest gift was his tremendous dramatic sensitivity. ("Theatrical" is the adjective most often applied to Puccini's work in comments both pro and con.) Or perhaps he simply realized that his chances for satisfaction and success lay in continuing Italian operatic tradition, rather than in creating pseudo-Wagnerian musical dramas. At any rate, quite undaunted by the fact that Massenet had already done so, Puccini settled on the Abbé Prévost's novel about the Chevalier de Grieux and Manon Lescaut as the plot for his next opera. Ricordi agreed to the idea and suggested Ruggiero Leoncavallo as librettist. Leoncavallo's work, however, proved unsatisfactory, and after two other authors also tried the job and gave it up, Ricordi thought that perhaps the well-known playwright Giuseppe Giacosa might be the man for the task. Giacosa, in his turn, asked the help of Luigi Illica, a man with some previous libretto-writing

* Between 1810 and 1829, Rossini composed thirty-eight operas—more than three times the number Puccini wrote in double the length of time.

experience. Giulio Ricordi himself did some writing for *Manon Lescaut*, not to mention arbitrating and pouring balm on the frequent heated disputes between the apparently impossible-to-satisfy Puccini and the often-despairing Illica and Giacosa. The result of all this was that when the opera was finally published, only Puccini's name appeared on it; none of the six librettists wanted any credit for his share in the work. *Manon Lescaut*, given on February 1, 1893 at the Teatro Regio in Turin, was an immediate success, and was promptly produced throughout Europe.

Exactly three years later, and on the same stage, *La Bohème* was first performed. Its conductor was new to the Teatro Regio, although he had already directed some of Puccini's work elsewhere. He was young, still in his twenties; his name was Arturo Toscanini.

Probably few libretti have caused as much difficulty as that of *La Bohème*. Versions of the story differ—(some even claim that the whole incident began and ended amicably)—but it seems almost certain that it was Puccini's decision to make an opera of the Murger sketches which caused his life-long enmity with Leoncavallo. This composer, whose *I Pagliacci* was a huge success from its 1892 première, apparently had made no secret of the fact that he was also working on an opera based on the French novel. Puccini and Leoncavallo both claimed precedence for the idea; Leoncavallo's *La Bohème* was produced a year after his rival's version, and because of the latter's growing popularity never attained much standing (although it was this opera that gave Caruso his first real start).

Puccini composed most of *La Bohème* at Torre del Lago, a Tuscan lakeside village where he had recently settled. Many of the decisions about the opera were made with Ricordi, Giacosa, and Illica by letter—a fact which hardly facilitated the work, nor eased its creators' doubts. At the same time that he worked on *La Bohème*, Puccini was also playing with an idea for another opera, *La Lupa* ("The She-Wolf"). Both librettists were angry that Puccini could berate them constantly for their slowness with the *La Bohème* work while not giving it his own full attention. Ricordi, who at first favored the *La Lupa* project, patiently soothed the irate tempers of all three men, and persuaded the librettists not to abandon the whole work, as they quite frequently wanted to do. (Giacosa later complained that a couple of *La Bohème* scenes cost him more paper and effort than any one of his own complete dramas.) Scenes and whole acts were written, revised, rewritten, and then abandoned completely. Mimi was killed countless times and ways before the final death scene was agreed on. Despite all the turmoil, Puccini was already toying with the idea of *Tosca* for his next opus; he actually went to Florence in the middle of the *La Bohème* work to watch Sarah Bernhardt in the Sardou drama.

Turin was chosen for the première of *La Bohème*, although other cities had also bid for it. The first performance of what would become one of the two or three, if not *the* best-loved of all operas was received with moderate enthusiasm by the audience and with reservations by the critics. But each subsequent performance aroused greater acclaim, and *La Bohème* became a huge popular favorite quite some time before the critics finally acknowledged that it probably *was* a masterpiece.

As with *La Vie de Bohème*, other composers had also decided that Sardou's successful play *La Tosca* would make good opera. But Ricordi favored Puccini for the job, and Illica and Giacosa were willing to write the libretto. (After all, their earlier work had been hugely successful, notwithstanding the agonies of its creation.) Puccini went to Paris to confer with Sardou; the latter was agreeable to the project. In fact, according to contemporary reports, the grand seigneur of the French stage became so enthusiastic about the whole idea of making an opera from his play that he offered innumerable suggestions on everything from dramatic sequences to stage props, and, apparently, eventually decided that he was personally responsible for the composition's very inception, not to mention the details of its entire production.

Tosca's première took place in Rome on January 14, 1900. The public liked it well enough, and, as with *La Bohème*, the more they heard it the better they liked it. Puccini's fame, by this time, was enough to bring foreign music critics as well as Italian into the opera house. The critics were divided about *Tosca*. Many professed great shock at the opera's mixture of gore, lust, love, and religion. Their views made little difference; *Tosca* strengthened the claims of those who saw Puccini as the successor to the aged Verdi; it is another of those works which are almost as essential to an opera company's success as the seats the audience sits in.

Again the nerve-wracking search for a libretto was on. Over and over Puccini would pounce on an idea only to discard it as unsatisfactory. Nervous and discouraged, he went to London to help produce one of his operas. Although he understood no English, Puccini seems to have been deeply impressed by a performance of Belasco's play *Madama Butterfly*, then playing in England. After returning to Italy and toying with other ideas, he finally inquired via Ricordi's American branch whether the Belasco play was available for an opera. Eventually he received a favorable answer and continued to fret while Illica and Giacosa began to build the libretto. Finally, however, the work of composing began—and abruptly halted when Puccini was badly hurt in an auto accident near Torre del Lago. (Motors, especially those attached to cars and boats, fascinated Puccini.) He was completely bedridden for many weeks, and for long months afterwards was confined to a wheelchair. But as soon as he could Puccini returned to *Madama Butterfly*, and the story of the little Japanese girl was finally scheduled for a gala première at La Scala in February 1904.

No expense was spared for this production. Tito Ricordi, Giulio's son, who had taken over most of his father's duties, himself attended and supervised rehearsals. Even Puccini, usually a pessimist about his own works, decided that this one would be a triumph. It was not. In fact, *Madama Butterfly* was as complete a failure as La Scala had entertained in some time.

Whatever was responsible for the fiasco—and there seems to be evidence that it was in large part the work of an organized anti-Puccini claque—the composer determined that *Madama Butterfly* would be a success. He revised it and divided the original overlong second act into what are now Acts II and III. By late spring, *Madama Butterfly* was ready to be presented again, this time at Brescia. It was a complete success and has remained one ever since.

Once more the search for a libretto began. Ideas were considered and rejected by the composer. In 1905, Puccini went to South America—his first trip outside Europe—to help stage his operas there. The next year Giacosa died, and Puccini felt his loss deeply. In January 1907, the composer sailed to New York at the invitation of the Metropolitan Opera's manager, Heinrich Conried, to supervise the productions of his works at the Met. New York society leaders made much of him during his stay; he also

(*Puccini nelle Immagini,* courtesy Rita Puccini)

Puccini as a struggling young musician in Milan.

(*Puccini nelle Immagini,* courtesy Rita Puccini)

Puccini's brother Michele.

(*Puccini nelle Immagini,* courtesy Rita Puccini)

Puccini, about the time he wrote *Le Villi*.

(*Puccini nelle Immagini,* courtesy Rita Puccini)

Puccini in 1900.

(*Puccini nelle Immagini,* courtesy Rita Puccini)

Puccini with his first librettist Ferdinando Fontana.

(*Puccini nelle Immagini,* courtesy Rita Puccini)

The composer Amilcare Ponchielli, Puccini's teacher at the Conservatory.

Major figures of Puccini's first Milan days.

(*Puccini nelle Immagini*)

The Piazza della Scala in Milan toward the end of the last century. The great opera house is at the left.

(*Puccini nelle Immagini*)

Represented from left to right: Verdi, Puccini, Arrigo Boito (standing), Pietro Mascagni, Ruggiero Leoncavallo (standing), and Umberto Giordano. Boito, the noted librettist and composer, was a leading backer of Puccini's first opera. Mascagni, composer of *Cavalleria Rusticana,* was Puccini's roommate at the Conservatory. Leoncavallo, composer of *I Pagliacci,* also wrote a Bohème opera that was overshadowed by Puccini's. Giordano wrote the opera *Andrea Chénier*.

(*Puccini nelle Immagini*, courtesy Rita Puccini)

Puccini's wife Elvira.

(*Puccini nelle Immagini,* courtesy Rita Puccini)

Puccini in his Torre del Lago villa with his wife and son.

(*Puccini nelle Immagini*)

Headquarters of the La Bohème Club at Torre del Lago.

(*Puccini nelle Immagini,* courtesy Rita Puccini)

Puccini (center) with Renato Simone (left) and Giuseppe Adami (right), the librettists of *Turandot*. Adami wrote also the librettos for *La Rondine* and *Il Tabarro*.

(*Puccini nelle Immagini,* courtesy Rita Puccini)

Puccini shortly before his death.

(*Puccini nelle Immagini*, courtesy Rita Puccini)

David Belasco, American playwright, author of *Madame Butterfly* and *The Girl of the Golden West*, on which Puccini's operas are based.

(*Puccini nelle Immagini*, courtesy Rita Puccini)

Victorien Sardou, noted French playwright, author of *Tosca*, on which Puccini's opera is based.

became acquainted with another Belasco play, *The Girl of the Golden West.*

Two new librettists, Carlo Zangarini and Guelfo Civinini, were chosen to turn Belasco's western thriller into Italian operatic form. The world première was given to the Metropolitan Opera, and Toscanini was chosen to conduct. The work was finished in 1910, and Puccini again sailed to New York to supervise the première. The opera itself was a dazzling success in New York—which is to say that the glittering cast (Caruso, Destinn, and Amato) was wildly applauded by a diamond-studded audience which had paid fabulous admission prices to be there. The critics were more reserved, and have kept their reservations; public enthusiasm also abated, and *La Fanciulla del West* never attained the popularity of the four operas preceding it. Although still given occasionally, it has never been a favorite.

Puccini's next undertaking was to be a comedy, commissioned by the Royal Opera of Vienna. But World War I halted musical negotiations between Austria and Italy, and Puccini asked a friend, Giuseppe Adami, to finish the libretto, already begun in German by two Viennese writers. The result, *La Rondine* ("The Swallow") was first performed during March 1917 in neutral Monte Carlo. It is Puccini's only work not published by the Ricordi firm. Puccini had never gotten along so well with Tito Ricordi as with the wise, patient, kindly, and paternal Giulio, whose death in 1912 had been another great loss. *La Rondine* was at first applauded by a war-weary audience; but its popularity waned, and it is now rarely presented.

Il Trittico ("The Triptych") was an operatic project which had interested Puccini for some time, and it was to this that he next turned. It consists of three one-act works, each quite different from the others. The libretti for two of the operas—*Gianni Schicchi* and *Suor Angelica*—were written by Giovacchino Forzano, a playwright. Adami wrote the third libretto, *Il Tabarro* ("The Cloak"). The latter is a melodrama of love and deception; but *Suor Angelica* and *Gianni Schicchi* represent Puccini's only attempts at a mystic and a comic subject, respectively. *Il Trittico* was first presented by the Metropolitan in New York in December 1918. *Gianni Schicchi* was instantly popular and has remained much more a favorite than the other two works.

In 1920, Puccini began work on his last—and, he hoped, his greatest—opera, *Turandot*. The eighteenth-century play had inspired others before him (one was Carl Maria von Weber). Its characters were unusual—more complex than those for whom Puccini had thus far composed; its setting was exotic; and the story had a quaint fairy-tale element, quite different from the rather earthy material of Puccini's previous works. Giuseppe Adami collaborated on the libretto with Renato Simoni, an eminent student of the theater. Puccini began on the music even before the libretto was finished. He worried about *Turandot's* perfection, which he felt was constantly just eluding him; he worried about growing old, and about an increasingly annoying constriction in his throat. In the fall of 1924, Puccini asked a doctor about his throat. The diagnosis was cancer; the composer was urged to go immediately for treatment to a clinic in Brussels, Belgium. He seemed to respond well to an operation performed there on November 24. But four days later he had a heart attack which was fatal within a few hours. Early in the morning of November 29, 1924, not quite 66 years old, Giacomo Puccini died.

The opera *Turandot* was completed by Franco Alfano, a well-known Italian composer and friend of Puccini. It was first conducted by Toscanini at La Scala on April 25, 1926. Today some consider it Puccini's finest work—as he wanted it to be.

Giacomo Puccini was a darkly handsome man, whose neat and dignified good looks increased with age. He was undoubtedly attractive to women, and the attraction was usually mutual. Both in Italy and during his American trips, Puccini's name was frequently coupled with that of one or another eligible lady, and he himself stated several times that he had to become enamoured of his own operatic heroines before they were alive enough for him to compose their music. When Puccini was twenty-five or twenty-six, he met Elvira Gemignani, wife of a Lucca merchant and mother of two small children. Elvira soon left her husband for Puccini, taking one of the children, her daughter Fosca, with her. Puccini loved the little girl, and their relationship was completely that of father and daughter. In 1886, Puccini's only son, Antonio, was born to Elvira.

Puccini and Elvira remained together most of the rest of his life. (She died in 1930). In 1903, when her legal husband Gemignani died, they were finally free to marry. Elvira was shy and did not particularly like the social limelight sometimes entailed by Puccini's status. But her chief fault was an almost pathological jealousy of Puccini. That he occasionally gave her ample cause for such jealousy was apparently quite true. But it was also true that her constant nagging doubts and accusations of Puccini led to frequent coldness and tension between them, and caused Puccini much personal misery.

Warm, fun-loving, and well-liked among intimates, Puccini never achieved the stature nor dignity of a Verdi. His refusal to take an overt pro-Ally stand in World War I caused a break with Toscanini; this was later healed, but their subsequent relationship consisted of periodic quarrels and lukewarm reconciliations. Though from boyhood moody and easily depressed, Puccini still enjoyed the often boisterous companionship of Torre del Lago's inhabitants. He liked to hunt with them on the lake and in the woods. A "La Bohème Club" was formed by his Torre del Lago friends; the club met in a hut, which contained an ancient piano where Puccini composed much of *La Bohème* while his friends sat drinking and joking. Puccini never lost his love for the natural surroundings and outdoor life of Torre del Lago. Even after fame made him a desired guest in Europe's fashionable drawing rooms, his letters expressed his desire to be away from the city and back at his lakeside home.

Puccini is remembered for almost always wearing a hat informally while he composed and rehearsed. He was constantly searching for plots to set to music, and he was conversant with most new musical trends of his time, although he did not have an intellectual approach to opera. His operatic characters are not introspective. Unhappy and restless unless he was actually working, Puccini was rarely completely satisfied with anything he composed. It was hard for him to put his ideas on paper; his manuscripts were sometimes so blotty and spotty that he scrawled in "Excuse me" especially for the copyists. Musically he borrowed from himself often; some of his themes are so characteristic that they spell "Puccini" no matter who sings them. But this makes little difference, for his music has direct emotional appeal. As long as operas are given anywhere, Puccini will be a well-loved name in the repertory.

THE LIBRETTISTS AND PUBLISHER

Illica, Giacosa, and Ricordi

Luigi Illica, the firebrand half of Puccini's long-suffering librettist team, was born in Castellarquato, Italy, in 1857. He died there in 1919. Between 1882 and 1892, Illica worked as a journalist in Milan, and also wrote numerous comedies and considerable poetry. Besides the four best-known Puccini operas on which he collaborated, Illica's work includes the libretti to Catalani's *La Wally*, (1892); Giordano's *Andrea Chenier*, (1896); Mascagni's *Iris*, (1898); and Franchetti's *Germania*, (1902). In all, he worked on more than fifty operatic libretti.

Giuseppe Giacosa, born in Colleretto Parella in 1847, originally studied to be a lawyer, as was his father. His first play, a verse drama produced in 1873, met with such success that he decided to become a full-time writer. His output was prolific: he wrote poetry; psychological, naturalistic, and bourgeois drama, in verse as well as prose (but few of his plays have been given in the United States); and impressionistic travel books. He is sometimes called typical of late nineteenth-century Italian dramatists. Giacosa was thoughtful and worked more slowly than his collaborator Illica. Greatly respected by both Puccini and the music publisher Ricordi, Giacosa died in 1906.

Librettists have been called "the forgotten men of opera"; the title might also be applied to music publishers, whose prize-contests, faith in unknown young composers, and forbearance with famous middle-aged ones have given the world operas that might otherwise have been killed before birth by the starvation and frustration of their creators.

(*Puccini nelle Immagini,* courtesy Rita Puccini)

Puccini with Giuseppe Giacosa and Luigi Illica, the librettists of *La Bohème, Manon Lescaut, Tosca,* and *Madama Butterfly.*

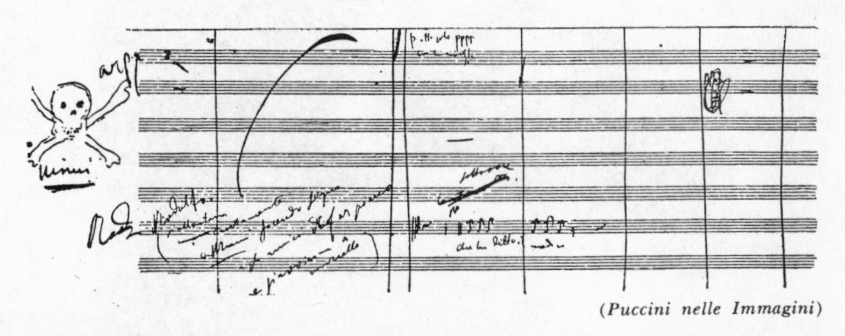

(*Puccini nelle Immagini*)

Sketch by Puccini in the autograph score of *La Bohème* at the moment of Mimi's death.

(*Puccini nelle Immagini,* courtesy Rita Puccini)

Giulio Ricordi, the great music publisher who stood behind Puccini from 1884 until his own death in 1912.

(*Puccini nelle Immagini,* courtesy Rita Puccini)

Tito Ricordi, Giulio's son and successor, in a costume reminiscent of the *Girl of the Golden West*.

Without Giulio Ricordi's musical acumen, generosity, and almost superhuman patience, Giacomo Puccini might have been compelled to return from Milan to the post of cathedral organist in Lucca. Giulio Ricordi possessed those character and personality traits of his father and grandfather which helped give the world many of the works of Bellini, Donizetti, Rossini, and Verdi.

Giovanni Ricordi, founder of the distinguished music-publishing House of Ricordi, was born in Milan in 1785. He began his career as an enterprising music copyist, soon adopted a mechanical method of copying, and in 1808 published the first score produced by this method in Italy. He knew Rossini and helped him maintain the rights to his works against would-be pirates; he published the operas of Bellini and Donizetti among others; he was the first to recognize the genius of Giuseppe Verdi (whose application for admission had previously been turned down by the Milan Conservatory). An unusually shrewd businessman, he expanded Casa Ricordi to include other musical items besides scores. Giovanni died in 1853, his confidence in his various protégés well justified and rewarded. He was succeeded by his son Tito. Tito, who had learned the business thoroughly from his father, introduced other new machines for the work of copying and printing scores, and continued to expand the firm. Branch offices were established, other publishers were bought out and absorbed, and in the 1880's Casa Ricordi became the most important music publisher in the world.

Tito's son Giulio—Puccini's friend and mentor—abandoned a promising military career to help his ailing father in the firm, and in 1887 took over completely. Giulio was himself a gifted and elegant composer (under the pen-name of "G. Burgmein"); he headed the Casa Ricordi's program of continuing expansion until his death in 1912, when the firm owned rights to and had published more than 112,000 compositions.

The last Ricordi to head the firm was Giulio's son Tito (1865–1933). He further increased Casa Ricordi's international operation before retiring from business in 1919. Though heavily bombed during World War II, the House of Ricordi made an amazing comeback, and today is once again a flourishing and leading international music-publishing organization.

MURGER AND LA VIE DE BOHÈME

Like Rodolphe in the book *La Vie de Bohème* (and Rodolfo in Act I of Puccini's opera), Henri Murger once edited a magazine named *Le Castor* ("The Beaver"). While modern romantics may picture this organ as a latter-day "little magazine," filled with the unappreciated (and underpaid) philosophic flights of Parisian intellectuals, its real function was much more prosaic: namely to be the trade journal of Parisian hatmakers. The resemblance between Murger and Rodolfo only begins with the editorship of "The Beaver", for much of Murger's *La Vie de Bohème* was autobiographical, and its other characters had real-life prototypes too.

Henri Murger, whose novel inspired Puccini's opera, was born in Paris in 1822, the son of a German immigrant who doubled as a *concierge* and tailor. Despite a disorganized education, Murger managed to become secretary to Count Alexei Tolstoy, a distant relation of Leo and a writer himself. Murger turned to journalism about 1841. His essays and poems, of necessity, were mixed with every other kind of writing he could get, so that he could earn enough to keep himself alive. It was at this time that he met and became one of the impoverished left-bank "Bohemians" whom he was to immortalize.

From 1845 to 1848 *La Vie de Bohème* appeared, serialized in a French periodical. Until it was adapted for the stage, the work did not bring Murger much income. In fact, the story is told, the playwright Barrière visited Murger's garret to discuss dramatizing the work. Murger was in bed, but denied being sick. Barrière suggested continuing their discussion at a café; Murger apologized for being unable to comply—he had, that morning, lent his only

(*Puccini nelle·Immagini,* courtesy Rita Puccini)

Henri Murger and three illustrations from the first edition of his novel *La Vie de Bohème.*

Rodolfo.

Mimi.

Musetta.

Marcello.

(*Puccini nelle Immagini*)

Original costume designs for *La Bohème,* water colors by Hohenstein.

pair of trousers to a friend, and was forced to wait in bed until the pants were returned.

Barrière's play, based on the book, appeared in 1849. It was successful and allowed Murger to take up a more comfortable style of living. Murger wrote several other works, but apparently weakened by his years of left-bank hardship, died in 1861.

At least one other character from *La Vie de Bohème* published memoirs describing the real-life people and places that Murger fictionalized. This person was Alexandre Schanne, better known as Schaunard, through a combination of nickname and printer's error. Schanne described the models (often more than one) for each of the other main characters. Though at the end of the book they are still the same struggling young Bohemians as at its beginning, Schanne mentions that most of them eventually achieved moderate financial success and a comfortable middle-class middle age, both in the arts and in business.

La Vie de Bohème is a witty and amusing series of related incidents in the lives of its main characters and their mistresses. Its epigrammatic style is a little like that of Thackeray or Wilde. Almost every chapter contains at least one episode, incident, or reference which occurs in Puccini's opera, but oddly enough, important elements for the opera's main plot—the affair of Rodolfo and Mimi, with the latter's death—are based on "Francine's Muff," a chapter of Murger which is not about the book's major characters but is, instead, a separate and sad little tale about the love and poverty of a sculptor named Jacques and a seamstress, Francine. The episode of the missing key in the first act occurs in this chapter (although in the book it is the girl who intentionally hides the key), and Francine's last wish—a muff for her cold hands—was given to Mimi. Another odd fact is that Murger's Mimi is a coldly selfish young lady whose actions were generally governed by calculated self-interest, whereas Musetta in the book is the gay, warm-hearted coquette. The tale of Schaunard and the parrot, almost buried in the confusion of Puccini's Act One, is told by Murger in one of the book's funniest chapters, "The Toilette of the Graces."

One of the earliest musical dramas based on the Murger-Barrière play was *La Petite Bohème*, an operetta by Henri Hirschmann, staged in Paris in 1877. Love not only conquers but also heals in this version, and Rodolfo's kisses revive the ailing Mimi.

Leoncavallo's operatic version of the book, produced in Venice, 1897, is more in the *verismo* (naturalistic) style than either Hirschmann's or Puccini's work. Marcello is the main character (and tenor). Act One takes place at the Café Momus; the four friends are about to be ejected for non-payment of their bill when Barbemuche, another character from Murger's book, comes to their aid. Leoncavallo's Act Two is set in the courtyard of Musetta's house. She has just been evicted but does not allow such a petty occurrence to interfere with a party, long before scheduled for that evening. The party takes place in the courtyard and ends in a glorious brawl between Musetta's Bohemian friends and her outraged neighbors. Act Three takes place in Marcello's garret, as Marcello and Rodolfo rid themselves respectively of Musetta and Mimi, who love them most of the time despite their poverty. In Act Four it is Christmas Eve in Rodolfo's studio; Mimi returns once more and dies in her lover's arms, to the accompaniment of the holiday chimes outside.

Various non-musical dramas based on Murger's novel also remained popular for more than a century after the book first appeared. A Clyde Fitch adaptation of Murger, called *The Bohemians*, opened in New York in March 1896, just one month after the world première of Puccini's opera. Mimi and Rodolfo were decorously wed at the end of the Fitch play, and somehow the landlord, Monsieur Benoit, was turned into Madame Benoit.

In 1916 a movie *La Vie de Bohème* appeared. Louella Parsons, reviewing it for the *Chicago Herald*, praised the film, although she sadly commented in her review that "Puccini's opera is woefully bereft of sunshine and smiles." Reading a plot summary of the movie forces one to the conclusion that any connection between it and either Murger *or* Puccini is indeed tenuous.

Other *La Bohème* movies have been made quite regularly, in fact almost every decade. The latest seems to be a 1946 French version. One interesting fact does arise from studying photographs of the various stage, film, and operatic productions which owe their origin to Murger: Rodolfo is always shown with abundant dark hair, although Murger distinctly described him as nearly bald.

SOME NOTES ON EARLY PERFORMANCES

In the less than three-score years since its Metropolitan Opera House première, *La Bohème* has been sung more than 360 times at the Metropolitan alone. It is just about tied with *Aida* as the opera most often given by the Metropolitan; *Carmen*, the runner-up, lags by almost a hundred performances.

In May 1897, in an article about a British performance of *La Bohème*, *New York Times* readers were assured that "New Yorkers need not be alarmed. They will not soon be confronted by these tunes they do not know." The *Times* was over-optimistic: *La Bohème* was being applauded throughout Europe, and it was only another year before New Yorkers were able to see it in their own city. The opera received a little-heralded New York première in Wallack's Theater on May 16, 1898. Actually, its first American performance had already taken place the previous October in Los Angeles!

By 1898 the *La Bohème* libretto had been translated into English, French, German, and Spanish; sizable selections of the music were available in an arrangement for full military band. It was on December 26, 1900, that *La Bohème* was finally performed on the Western Hemisphere's leading opera stage, the Metropolitan. Other operas in the repertory that season included Wagner, Balfe's *Bohemian Girl* (no relation to *La Bohème*), and works by Meyerbeer, Massenet, and Gilbert and Sullivan. Those were the days of regular Sunday night gala performances, and an ordinary evening's fare might be a double bill of *La Traviata* and *Cavalleria Rusticana*. Nellie Melba, who agreed with those who called her the greatest diva of the opera stage, sang Mimi at the *La Bohème* première. She was forty years old and still at her peak. Reviewers found that she sang the part "clearly . . . beautifully and soullessly." (Also from the *Times.*) Melba's appearances were enthusiastically received. Toward the end of the 1900–01 season, she rewarded her admirers at the Metropolitan by following her performance of Mimi with the entire Mad Scene from *Lucia di Lammermoor.*

Though it aroused no critical acclaim, *La Bohème* was found significant enough to stimulate articles and comments in leading American and European magazines. The authors of these remarks were usually in sad disagreement with one another. An English music critic of 1896, discussing the opera's world première, found the music "by no means deficient in merit [but] hampered by an ineffective libretto." The critic dutifully upheld Victorian propriety in the statement that "Murger's *La Vie de Bohème* [is] hardly suitable for the book of an opera."

On the other hand, the *New York Times* of December 27, 1900, reviewing the preceding night's Metropolitan opera première of *La Bohème,* called the libretto "tolerably good opera book . . . the music . . . clever . . . but less so than the book." The *Times* reviewer goes on to deplore the "Offenbachian" comedy of Act Two, and sighs for a return to grand opera as exemplified in *Aida.*

The French disagreed with both these views and found Murger's *La Vie de Bohème* ideally suited for the book of an opera, and *La Bohème* the supreme example of Puccini's talent. A June 1898 article in the Parisian journal *L'Illustration* also mentioned that Puccini was just then engaged in turning Sardou's play *La Tosca* into an opera; this venture, the author declared, was sure to be as great a success as Puccini's preceding two operas, since the composer used French sources for his inspiration.

In April 1901, *Musical World* reprinted a *New York Times* article by that newspaper's music critic, W. J. Henderson. Henderson admitted that the audience rather seemed to enjoy the Puccini opera, commented on the unfortunate frequency of consumption among operatic heroines, and ended his article with a thoughtful judgment: "Nevertheless, we cannot believe that there is permanent success for an opera constructed as this one is."

Eighteen years and one-hundred-and-one Metropolitan performances later, even the most conservative critics had to admit that *La Bohème* was gaining on them. The renowned Henry

(*Puccini nelle Immagini*)

Evan Gorga, the first Rodolfo, in costume.

(*Puccini nelle Immagini,* courtesy Rita Puccini)

Cesira Ferrani, the first Mimi, in costume.

Nellie Melba, the Mimi at the Metropolitan Opera première.

Alma Gluck as Mimi.

Famous singers of the past connected with *La Bohème.*

Alexandre Schanne, model for Murger's Schaunard.

Arturo Toscanini, who conducted the world première of *La Bohème*.

(Courtesy Sadler's Wells Opera)

Australian soprano Elizabeth Fretwell in the role of Musetta.

(Courtesy San Francisco Opera Association)

Salvatore Baccaloni in the role of Alcindoro.

Edward Krehbiel, a cautious man, wrote that "Even those who feel disposed to be moralists when they sit in the theater have accustomed themselves to hear . . . *La Bohème* without moral retchings."

La Bohème is not philosophical music drama along the lines of *Goetterdaemmerung*. It lacks *Il Trovatore's* situations for sensational vocal performances. Puccini—as happens with most great artists, regardless of their metier—periodically is thought "unfashionable." Nevertheless, it looks as if *La Bohème* is here to stay.

PLOT SUMMARY

Act One

Characters in order of their appearance in this act:
Marcello and Rodolfo; Colline; Schaunard; Benoit; Mimi

La Bohème takes place in Paris about 1830. Act One begins with a brief orchestral prelude as the curtain rises on a large shabby, sparsely furnished garret. On one side is a sloping skylight; on the other, a few chairs, a table, cupboard, and bed. Rodolfo, the poet, stares out the skylight, blows on his hands, and stamps his feet in a vain attempt to get warm. Marcello, the painter, is at work behind an easel. His picture is called "The Passage of the Red Sea"; and Marcello speaks first, declaring that he is as cold as though the Red Sea were running down his back, icy drop by drop.

Asked what *he* is doing, Rodolfo replies that he is watching the smoke from other chimneys and thinking what an idle wretch their own stove is. Half jokingly, they complain back and forth until Marcello, unable to paint any longer, puts down his brush. His fingers are as frozen, he says, as if he were still holding them against the heart of his erstwhile love, Musetta.

Marcello wants to break up a chair for firewood, but Rodolfo has a better idea. They will burn his unpublished masterpiece, a play. Banteringly, they commit the manuscript to the stove and are warming themselves from its fire when Colline, the philosopher, enters.

Surely the end of the world is at hand, Colline snorts. He has just tried to pawn some books, but because it is Christmas Eve, the pawnshops are closed. Seeing the blaze, he inquires about its source and commends the author on the fieriness of his work.

Just as Rodolfo's play has all too quickly burned down, two boys enter with food, wine, cigars, and firewood. They are followed by the fourth friend, Schaunard, a musician, who gaily scatters coins about. The others are so excited by the unaccustomed luxuries, so busy rekindling the stove and setting the table, that they pay no attention at all to Schaunard's rambling tale of his sudden wealth. But the musician stops them before they can eat, and reminds them it is Christmas Eve. They may drink at home, says Schaunard, but they must eat out—for Paris is gay tonight, and its streets are filled with festive crowds.

The friends are pouring wine when a knock on the door announces Benoit, their landlord, coming for his rent. Benoit is plied with wine and teased about a recent romantic exploit. But when he mentions having a wife, the young men, in mock horror at their landlord's immorality, eject him from the room. They then divide Schaunard's money and prepare to go to the Café Momus.

Rodolfo says he will meet them downstairs; he still wants to finish an article he has been writing. Urging him to hurry, the others depart. The poet tries to work when another knock and a timid apology proclaim an unknown girl outside. It is Mimi—her candle has gone out, and she would like to borrow a light.

Rodolfo opens the door and motions the girl inside. Mimi, pale and nearly fainting, drops both her candle and her key. The poet urges her to sit for a moment until she feels better and gives her some wine. Revived, Mimi takes the candle Rodolfo picks up and lights for her; but as she is leaving, she remembers having dropped her key. She stands in the draughty doorway wondering where the key fell, and her candle goes out again.

Rodolfo comes towards her with a fresh light, but the draught extinguishes this also. The two grope on the floor in the dark, looking for Mimi's key. Rodolfo cheerfully brushes aside the girl's repeated apologies. He finds the key, slyly pockets it, and pretends to continue searching. In the dark, he manages to touch Mimi's hand, and now the three most famous songs of Act One follow each other in rapid succession.

"Che gelida manina!" ("What a frozen little hand!") Rodolfo exclaims, and asks Mimi if she would like to know who he is and what he does. He is a poet, he tells her in this aria, known as "Rodolfo's Narrative"; poor, but with a millionaire's soul, and a weakness for beautiful eyes—like Mimi's. Her presence is more lovely than any of his daydreams; and now that she knows his story, wouldn't she like to tell him about herself?

"Sì"—"Yes"—says Mimi, and does so. "Mi chiamano Mimì" ("They call me Mimi"), she begins. She is his neighbor, an embroiderer who likes best to stitch flowers that remind her of springtime. She lives alone and eagerly looks forward to the warmth and sunshine of April. She regrets that her embroidered flowers lack the perfume of real ones—and that is about all there is to tell of herself.

Rodolfo is greatly touched by Mimi's sweetness and simplicity. When shouts from his friends outside urge him to hurry and join them, he calls back that he is not alone—to go along and he will meet them later—and Marcello, Schaunard, and Colline depart singing.

The poet turns to see Mimi standing in the moonlight, and in the duet beginning "O Soave Fanciulla" ("Oh gentle girl") sings of the love already stirring in him. Mimi half yields to his kiss, changes her mind, and suddenly becoming coquettish, asks if she might come with him to meet his friends. Rodolfo hints how much nicer it would be to stay right there, but Mimi assures him she will remain close to him anyway. Rodolfo gallantly offers her his arm, and they leave, still singing of their new love. Act One ends with the moon illuminating the now-deserted garret, while Mimi's and Rodolfo's duet fades into the distance.

Act Two

Characters in order of their appearance in this act:
Schaunard; Colline; Rodolfo and Mimi; Marcello; Parpignol; Musetta and Alcindoro

The second act takes place a short time later that evening in a crowded, busy, noisy square in the Latin Quarter. On one side is the Café Momus; on the other, a variety of stalls and small shops. Vendors, hawkers, students, shop-girls, street arabs, sightseers—to all appearances, the larger part of the population of Paris—mill about, shouting, laughing, gesticulating, and jostling one another. The hawkers and vendors noisily proclaim their wares; children follow them, mimicking their cries. Disjointed comments from persons in the crowd mingle with their shouts. The whole impression is one of colorful, gay, noisy confusion. Schaunard dickers with a vendor over a toy horn; Colline transacts some business with a clothes-mender at one of the stalls; Rodolfo and Mimi, engrossed in each other, wander on the fringes of the crowd, and look at shop windows; and Marcello walks about and flirts with various pretty girls.

Against the constant background of hawkers' cries and general noise, Rodolfo and Mimi enter a milliner's to buy a bonnet; the other three friends, with a few profound comments on the nature of crowds, disappear into the Momus and re-emerge, carrying a table and followed by a waiter with chairs. At this point delighted yells announce the approach of the toy merchant Parpignol, who is immediately surrounded by a mob of enthusiastic children. Frantic mothers at first try to retrieve their offspring from the crowd around Parpignol; finding their efforts less than successful, the mothers finally give in to their children's noisy wishes and buy the desired toys. Parpignol and his followers depart. Rodolfo and Mimi, resplendent in her new bonnet, join the other three at their table. Rodolfo introduces Mimi who is gravely welcomed into the company, and the important business of ordering dinner begins.

Wine is brought, and the friends raise their glasses in a toast. They are about to drink when Marcello loudly demands poison: he has just seen his former (but not forgotten) mistress Musetta, who, with the elderly and dandified Alcindoro trotting behind, makes her way through the crowd to the sound of admiring "Ohs" and "Ahs." Musetta cleverly selects a just-vacated table right beside the one at which the friends sit, and proceeds, not too subtly, to flirt with Marcello. He, however, stonily keeps his back to her. Mimi, curious as to the newcomer's identity, hears a few unflattering things about her from Marcello; and Musetta, a bit piqued at being ignored, relieves her frustration somewhat by smashing a plate. Alcindoro frantically implores her to watch her manners; Colline and Schaunard comment happily on the situation; Mimi sympathizes with "poor" Musetta and assures Rodolfo of her own undying fidelity; and Musetta, finding her efforts thus far unrewarded, breaks into her waltz song, "Quando me'n vò" ("Whenever I walk") which she obviously addresses to Marcello, although his back is still turned to her.

In this lilting song, Musetta tells of the admiration and desire her beauty arouses among menfolk wherever she goes (a condition quite to her taste). As she sings, Alcindoro continues begging her to behave herself: what will People say??? Marcello, pushed almost beyond endurance, gets up to leave, but is rooted to the spot by Musetta's voice; Mimi sympathizes with Musetta; Rodolfo in vain tries to explain the situation to her; and Schaunard and Colline enjoy the comedy from the sidelines.

Her song ended, Musetta decides that it is time to get rid of Alcindoro. She suddenly discovers her shoe to be unbearably tight and painful: nothing will do but that the elderly swain go to the bootmaker's immediately and buy another pair. Alcindoro fussily trots off; Marcello, his resistance at last overcome, and Musetta joyously embrace each other; and the waiter unexpectedly appears with the bill, which nobody seems able to pay, Schaunard's money having mysteriously vanished.

Musetta breezily tells the waiter to present both bills to Alcindoro when he returns. The others echo her words in happy amazement. Fanfare, drums, and the excited crowd announce the approach of a parade of soldiers, who enter led by a baton-twirling drum major. Musetta, unable to walk in only one shoe, is carried off behind the parade by Marcello and Colline. Schaunard follows, blaring away on his new horn; Rodolfo and Mimi go next, arm in arm; and Act Two ends to band music, just as Alcindoro re-enters with the new shoes, and is presented with the combined bills.

Act Three

Characters in order of their appearance in this act:
Tollgate sergeant; Mimi; Marcello; Rodolfo; Musetta

Act Three takes place the following February, just before dawn on a bitter cold morning. The scene is outside an inn by one of the tollgates into Paris.

Over the inn door hangs Marcello's painting "The Passage of the Red Sea," now clearly labeled "At the Port of Marseilles." The walls of the inn are decorated with pictures of a Turk and a Zouave. A few bare trees and benches occupy the space between inn and tollgate. Some street cleaners, shivering with cold, bang brooms and pails on the tollgate and are finally admitted by a sleepy official. Sounds of revelry come from the inn, and Musetta's voice, in an echo of her waltz song, rises above the others. Carters and peasants pass into the city with their wares as the bleak winter day gradually breaks. Mimi comes out through the tollgate; as she nears the inn, she has a violent coughing spell. Finally managing to control it, she asks the gatekeeper if this is where the painter works. Told it is, Mimi begs a woman who has come from the inn to fetch Marcello. She herself waits outside as various other people come out of the inn and along the road through the barrier into Paris.

Marcello emerges from the inn. Surprised to see Mimi, he urges her to enter, but she refuses and pleads for his help. Rodolfo loves her, she says, but his jealousy is driving her to distraction. Marcello gently suggests a separation as the best solution and points through the window to Rodolfo inside. The poet came to the inn just that night and fell asleep on a bench. Mimi, suppressing another coughing attack, gasps that Rodolfo musn't see her here. She hides on the side as Rodolfo comes out.

As Mimi creeps nearer to listen, Rodolfo also tells Marcello of his wish to separate from the girl. Marcello agrees it is wise, but reminds the poet that he is not entirely without faults himself. Rodolfo complains of Mimi's flirtatiousness; then admits that despite it all, he still loves her and is dreadfully worried about her: she grows weaker daily and has a terrible cough. Marcello tries to keep Rodolfo out of Mimi's earshot, but she moves closer in order to hear. Realizing how ill she is, Mimi weeps bitterly until her sobbing and coughing reveal her presence.

A loud laugh from Musetta resounds from the Inn. Marcello rushes inside to see what is happening. Mimi bids Rodolfo a sad farewell ("Addio senza rancor"), and tells him she'll send the porter for her few effects; if he would like to keep as a remembrance the bonnet he once gave her, he should do so. She even manages to joke a little as Rodolfo recalls their past happiness.

They are looking forward to the coming spring's warmth, when, to the accompaniment of breaking dishes, the voices of Musetta and Marcello are heard quarreling. The latter two rush from the inn hurling recriminations at each other and continue their brawling outdoors. A quartet follows: Marcello and Musetta shout furious insults at each other, while Mimi and Rodolfo, softened by their memories and the thought of the approaching springtide, decide to stay together until the season of flowers. The act ends as Marcello storms back into the inn, Musetta stamps off in another direction, and Mimi and Rodolfo, temporarily reconciled, move away arm in arm.

Act Four

Characters in order of appearance in this act:
Marcello and Rodolfo; Schaunard and Colline; Musetta; Mimi

Act Four takes place some months later in the same garret as Act One. Once again, Marcello is behind his easel, trying to paint; Rodolfo makes a half-hearted attempt to write. The poet is telling Marcello that he has seen Musetta, splendidly dressed and riding in a carriage. Marcello feebly expresses pleasure at the news, but Rodolfo, in an aside, doubts the painter's sincerity. Marcello has similar news about Mimi; and when Rodolfo pretends joy at Mimi's good fortune, the painter, in his turn, is equally dubious.

Neither young man can work. Each furtively kisses a memento left behind by his mistress, and they sing a plaintive duet about their lost loves ("Ah Mimi, tu più non torni"). But they rouse themselves just as Schaunard and Colline enter, bringing rolls and a herring; and once more, a spirit of fun takes over.

A bottle of water is placed in Colline's hat with the explanation that the champagne is going on ice. The meager food is passed around as diverse tempting delicacies. Schaunard refuses the fare, explaining that he must attend a dance that night; and Colline pompously announces that the king awaits him. Schaunard suggests a dance, and after some debate, a quadrille is chosen;

(Courtesy Sadler's Wells Opera.
Photo by Houston Rogers)

Rosanna Carteri.

(Courtesy San Francisco Opera Association)

Anna Moffo.

(Courtesy London Records.
Photo by Fayer, Vienna)

Renata Tebaldi.

(Courtesy San Francisco Opera Association)

Dorothy Kirsten.

Contemporary sopranos in the role of Mimi.

(*Puccini nelle Immagini,* courtesy Rita Puccini)

Page from the autograph score. Mimi sings, "But when the thaw comes the first sunshine is mine" (Act I).

Rodolfo bows to Marcello, who, in a coy falsetto, begs the gentleman to respect "her" modesty. Colline and Schaunard pretend to quarrel violently, seize tongs and poker from the fireplace, and prepare to duel to the death.

As the fun is at its peak, the door bursts open and an agitated Musetta rushes in. Mimi is outside, she says, too weak to climb the remaining stairs. Rodolfo and Marcello help Mimi in and place her on the bed Colline and Schaunard drag forward. While Rodolfo tends Mimi, Musetta tells the others how she sought and found the girl, whose only wish was to die near Rodolfo. Mimi and her lover are overjoyed to see each other again, but the others deplore their poverty: they have nothing to give Mimi, who, they see, has only a short time to live.

Mimi drowsily wishes for a muff: her hands are so cold. Musetta removes her earrings and gives them to Marcello. Sell them, she tells him, buy medicine and bring a doctor; she herself will fetch the muff. They go. Schaunard and Colline have been watching the scene sadly and quietly. Now Colline takes off his well-loved old coat and sings a touching farewell to it ("Vecchia zimarra") as he prepares to sell it. He then reminds Schaunard that it would be an act of mercy to leave Mimi and Rodolfo alone. Schaunard takes the water bottle to justify his departure and leaves with Colline.

Mimi rouses herself and tells Rodolfo she was only pretending to sleep so that she might be alone with him. She is still as lovely as the dawn, the poet says, but she corrects him: lovely as the sunset would be a better simile. She is delighted that he has kept and cherished her bonnet. Together they recall the events of their first meeting on Christmas Eve. Musical phrases from the first and third acts form the background for this scene.

Exhausted by a coughing spasm, Mimi falls back on the bed as Schaunard re-enters, followed by Musetta with the muff and Marcello with medicine. Mimi takes the muff with childish delight, begs the grief-stricken Rodolfo not to weep, and quietly falls asleep.

Musetta, murmuring a prayer, shades the lamp and heats the medicine; Rodolfo frequently steals to the bed to look at Mimi. A ray of sunshine falls through the skylight on Mimi. Marcello and Schaunard tiptoe to the bedside, see that Mimi is dead, and start back in alarm. Musetta signals Rodolfo to screen the skylight with her cloak. Colline enters and helps Rodolfo; Musetta motions that the medicine is ready. Just then the poet notices the strange behaviour of Marcello and Schaunard, and asks its meaning. Unable to hide the truth any longer, Marcello embraces Rodolfo with a word of sympathy. Rodolfo, realizing what has happened, throws himself across the bed with a wild cry "Mimi!" Musetta bursts into tears; and the others stand sorrowfully and silently as the curtain falls on *La Bohème*.

MUSICAL THEMES

As a Conservatory student in Milan, Puccini became familiar with Wagner's music. He himself used a sort of *leitmotif* technique, which is quite evident in *La Bohème*.

A *leitmotif* (the term, which means "leading motive," was first used in describing Wagner's "Ring" cycle about the time Puccini's operatic career began) is a particular musical phrase or theme that always stands for a certain character or situation. Fully developed, the *leitmotif* music is an important part of an opera's major arias and orchestral interludes. But *leitmotifs* are also the listener's guide to the emotional climate of an opera. By varying the harmony and orchestration of a theme, the composer sets the mood for the action on stage.

Puccini used the same sequences throughout *La Bohème*; but by subtle changes in their musical construction those phrases that first indicated fun and gaiety later foreshadow sadness and death. Acts One and Two of *La Bohème* are comic; Acts Three and Four move steadily toward the final tragedy. Act Four recapitulates melodies heard throughout the rest of the opera, but the recapitulations differ from the original versions: music that formerly conveyed humor and playfulness now suggests the pathos of Mimi's hopeless situation.

Act One of *La Bohème* begins with the brief theme that stands for the Bohemian friends together. The same music heralds first Schaunard's entrance, then old Benoit's. The theme is repeated when Marcello, Schaunard, and Colline depart for the Momus while Rodolfo stays behind to write his article; and again before the duet "O Soave Fanciulla," when the other three, offstage, urge Rodolfo to hurry and join them. In Act Three the "Bohemian" music is heard when Marcello and Rodolfo come out of the tavern. In the last act it again serves as a brief interlude and announces the arrival of Schaunard (as well as his eventual departure with Colline). In Act Four this theme changes from a brassy, vivacious tune to a rather hollow imitation of itself.

Rodolfo is introduced in Act One by one of those melodies that are unmistakably Puccini. The music of this phrase ("Nei cieli bigi") is repeated in "Rodolfo's Narrative"; and, of course, some of the latter's melody is carried into "O Soave Fanciulla." Rodolfo's theme is heard often throughout Act One: for example, when the manuscript is burned; when the poet is on the stage alone just before Mimi's entrance. The Rodolfo music occurs in Act Two as Mimi and Rodolfo join the others at the Café. It announces his presence in Act Three; and, of course, snatches of it occur in the opera's last act, where part of "Rodolfo's Narrative" is sung by the dying Mimi as she pathetically recalls her first happy meeting with the poet.

Mimi's own theme, gay and lighthearted during her Act One entrance, becomes ominous and foreboding in the third and fourth acts. In Act Three Mimi's theme sustains the impression of bleakness and bitter cold which is so aptly made by the hollow opening chords of this act. In Act Four a segment of the Mimi music occurs when Marcello first tells of having seen the girl. Later it seems to warn listeners of what is going to happen before the actors themselves become aware of it. Each repetition of the theme increases the suggestion of doom and hopelessness.

Puccini was a master at conveying dramatic meaning via musical innuendo. Though his music has been criticized for its theatricality and frequent repetitiveness, it is these very qualities which give his operas so much of their appeal and dramatic impact.

La Bohème contains seven major "set" pieces—i.e. arias and ensembles. These are:

Act One

"Che gelida manina" ("Rodolfo's Narrative")—sung by Rodolfo

"Mi chiamano Mimì"—sung by Mimi

"O soave fanciulla"—sung by Rodolfo and Mimi

Act Two

"Quando me'n vò" (Musetta's waltz-song)—sung by Musetta

Act Three

"Addio senza rancor"—sung by Mimi

Act Four

"Mimi, tu più non torni"—sung by Rodolfo and Marcello

"Vecchia zimarra"—sung by Colline

Puccini. Caricature by Caruso. From *Caricatures by Enrico Caruso*, published by "La Follia di New York," 1922. Courtesy of the publisher.

Caruso himself as Rodolfo. Viafora as Mimi. Antonio Scotti as Marcello.

Caricatures by Caruso. From *Caricatures by Enrico Caruso*, published by "La Follia di New York," 1922. Courtesy of the publisher.

Adamo Didur as Schaunard. Pini-Corsi as Benoit. Andreas De Segurola as Colline.

Caricatures by Caruso. From *Caricatures by Enrico Caruso,* published by "La Follia di New York," 1922. Courtesy of the publisher.

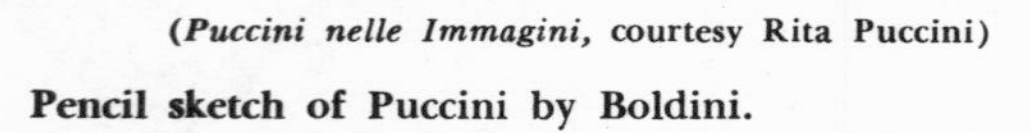

(*Puccini nelle Immagini*, courtesy Rita Puccini)

Pencil sketch of Puccini by Boldini.

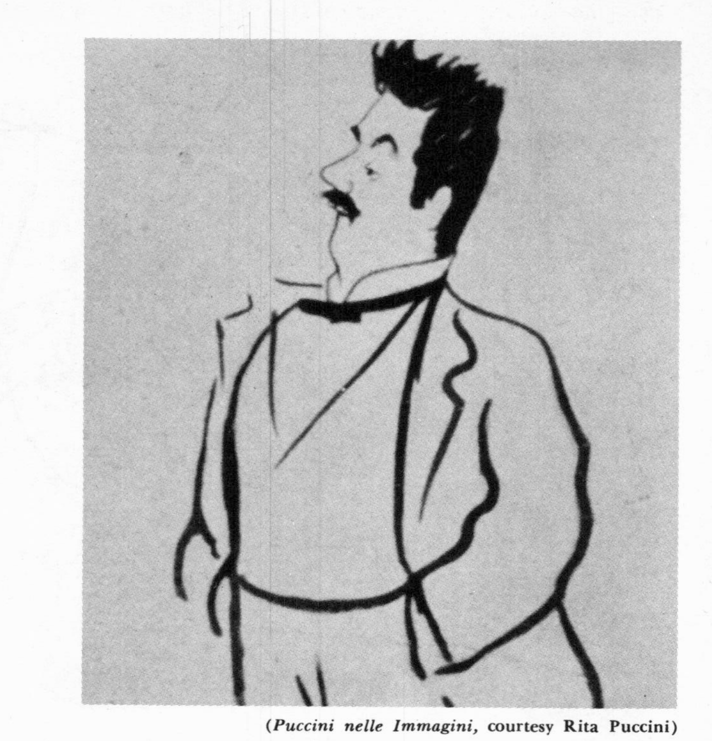

(*Puccini nelle Immagini*, courtesy Rita Puccini)

Caricature of Puccini by A. Neri.

LA BOHÈME

Opera in Four Acts

Music by Giacomo Puccini

Libretto by Giuseppe Giacosa and Luigi Illica

LA BOHÈME

Major characters, in order of appearance and in relationship to one another:

The Four Bohemians

MARCELLO, a painter, and best friend to Rodolfo	Baritone
RODOLFO, a poet	Tenor
COLLINE, a philosopher	Bass
SCHAUNARD, a musician	Baritone
BENOIT, the landlord	Bass
MIMI, an embroiderer who becomes Rodolfo's mistress	Soprano
PARPIGNOL, a toy vendor	Tenor
MUSETTA, off-again on-again mistress to Marcello	Soprano
ALCINDORO, Musetta's elderly and pompous admirer	Bass
TOLLGATE SERGEANT	Bass

Students, shop-girls, hawkers, vendors, mothers, children, and other members of crowd; sweepers, peasants, stragglers, etc.

ACT ONE

(Courtesy Gran Teatro del Liceo, Barcelona)

Setting for Act 1.

ACT ONE

Paris, the Latin Quarter. Christmas Eve, circa 1830.
Scene: A garret. On one side, a large sloping skylight. On the other side, a door leading to the staircase; another door. Table, chairs, bed, cupboard, wood-burning stove, etc.
The curtain rises quickly to a short prelude.
RODOLFO, the poet, is staring out the window.
MARCELLO, the painter, works at his easel. Both frequently shift position, blow on their hands, and stamp their feet.

MARCELLO: Questo Mar Rosso mi ammollisce e assidera come se addosso mi piovesse in stille.	This Red Sea wears me down and chills me as if it were raining upon me drop by drop.
Regards painting critically.	
Per vendicarmi affogo un Faraon.	In order to revenge myself, I'll drown a Pharaoh.
To Rodolfo.	
Che fai?	What are you doing?
RODOLFO: Nei cieli bigi guardo fumar dai mille comignoli Parigi—	I'm looking in the gray skies at the smoke from thousands of Parisian chimneys—
Points to unlit stove.	
—e penso a quel poltrone d'un vecchio caminetto ingannatore che vive in ozio come un gran signor.	—and thinking of that old deceitful sluggard of a stove, living in leisure like a grand lord.
MARCELLO: Le sue rendite oneste da un pezzo non riceve.	It hasn't received its just dues for a good while.

RODOLFO: Quelle sciocche foreste, che fan sotto la neve?	Those stupid forests, what good are they under the snow?
MARCELLO: Rodolfo, io voglio dirti un mio pensier profondo: Ho un freddo cane.	Rodolfo, I want to tell you one of my profound thoughts: I'm a frozen dog.
RODOLFO: Ed io, Marcello, non ti nascondo, che non credo al sudor della fronte.	And I, Marcello, won't hide from you that I've no faith in the sweat of my brow.
MARCELLO: Ho ghiacciate le dita quasi ancor le tenessi immollate giù in quella gran ghiacciaia che è il cuore di Musetta.	My fingers are almost as frozen as if I were still holding them sunk into that big chunk of ice which is Musetta's heart.

Sighs and puts down paintbrush.

RODOLFO: L'amor è un caminetto che sciupa troppo.	Love is a stove that eats too much.
MARCELLO: E in fretta.	And too fast.
RODOLFO: Dove l'uomo è fascina—	Where the man is the faggot—
MARCELLO: —e la donna è l'alare.	—and the woman is the andiron.
RODOLFO: L'uno brucia in un soffio—	The one burns up in a flash—
MARCELLO: —e l'altro sta guardare.	—and the other stands and watches.
RODOLFO: Ma intanto qui si gela.	But meanwhile, it's freezing here.
MARCELLO: E si muore d'inedia!	And I'm dying of starvation!
RODOLFO: Fuoco ci vuole.	We need a fire.
MARCELLO: Aspetta!	Wait!

He grabs a chair and tries to break it.

Sacrifichiam la sedia!	Let's sacrifice the chair!
RODOLFO: Eureka!	Eureka!

Rushes to stop Marcello.

MARCELLO: Trovasti?	You've found something?
RODOLFO: Sì!	Yes!

Fetches a thick manuscript from the table.

Aguzza l'ingegno! L'idea vampi in fiamma. . . .	My genius is aroused. Let the idea burst into flame. . . .
MARCELLO: Bruciamo il Mar Rosso?	Are we going to burn the Red Sea?

He points to his painting.

RODOLFO: No. Puzza la tela di pinta. Il mio dramma, l'ardente mio dramma ci scaldi.	No. The canvas will stink of paint. My drama, my fiery drama will warm us.
MARCELLO: Vuoi leggerlo forse? Mi geli.	You want to read it, perhaps? It will freeze me.
RODOLFO: No, in cener la carta si sfaldi e l'estro rivoli a suoi cieli. Al secol gran danno minaccia, è Roma in periglio!	No, the manuscript will turn to ashes page by page, and my poetic frenzies shall re-ascend to their heavens. Their loss threatens the century, and Rome totters!

Pompously hands a section of the manuscript to Marcello.

MARCELLO: Gran cuor!	Great heart!
RODOLFO: A te, l'atto primo.	For you, the first act.
MARCELLO: Qua.	Here.
RODOLFO: Straccia.	Tear it up.
MARCELLO: Accendi.	You light it.

Rodolfo strikes a flint and lights a fire in the stove.

RODOLFO: Che lieto baglior!	What a gay blaze!

MARCELLO: Che lieto baglior!	What a gay blaze!

They gleefully warm themselves as Colline enters, angrily tossing a bundle of books on the table.

COLLINE: Già dell'Apocalisse appariscono i segni. In giorno di vigilia non s'accettano pegni . . . una fiammata!	The signs of the Apocalypse are truly apparent. On Christmas Eve they won't accept pawn pledges . . . a fire!
RODOLFO: Zitto, si dà il mio dramma . . .	Quiet, my play is being given. . .
COLLINE: . . . al fuoco. Lo trovo scintillante.	. . . to the fire. I find it sparkling.
RODOLFO: Vivo.	Vivid.

The fire diminishes.

COLLINE: Ma dura poco.	But it's very short.
RODOLFO: La brevità, gran pregio.	Brevity is a great merit.
COLLINE: Autore, a me la sedia.	Author, give me your chair.

Takes Rodolfo's chair.

MARCELLO: Quest'intermezzi fan morir d'inedia. Presto.	These intermissions will make me die of starvation. Hurry up.

Rodolfo puts more manuscript on the fire.

RODOLFO: Atto secondo.	Second act.
MARCELLO: Non far susurro. . .	Don't make a sound. . .
COLLINE: Pensier profondo. . .	Profound thought. . .
MARCELLO: Giusto color!	True color!

They warm themselves.

RODOLFO: In quell'azzurro guizzo languente sfuma un'ardente scena d'amor!	An ardent love scene is consumed in that lazy blue smoke!
COLLINE: Scoppietta un foglio.	A page is crackling.

MARCELLO: Là c'eran baci!	Those were kisses there!
RODOLFO: Tre atti or voglio d'un colpo udir.	Now I want to hear three acts at one stroke.
COLLINE: Tal degli audaci l'idea s'integra.	Thus is an idea born among the daring.
RODOLFO, MARCELLO, COLLINE: Bello in allegra vampa svanir.	How lovely to vanish in a cheery flame.
MARCELLO: Oh! Dio . . . già s'abbassa la fiamma.	Oh! Lord . . . the flame is already going down.
COLLINE: Che vano, che fragile dramma!	What an empty, what a frail drama!
MARCELLO: Già scricchiola, increspasi, muor!	Already it's crackling, it's curling up, dying!
COLLINE and MARCELLO: Abbasso, abbasso, l'autor!	Down, down with the author!

Enter two boys bearing trays of food, firewood, etc.

RODOLFO: Legna!	Wood!
MARCELLO: Sigari!	Cigars!
COLLINE: Bordò!	Bordeaux!
RODOLFO: Legna!	Wood!
MARCELLO: Bordò!	Bordeaux!
RODOLFO, MARCELLO, COLLINE: Le dovizie d'una fiera il destin ci destinò.	Fate has sent us the riches of a whole market!

Enter Schaunard, scattering coins.

SCHAUNARD: La banca di Francia per voi si sbilancia.	The Bank of France declares in your favor.
COLLINE: Raccatta, raccatta!	Pick them up, pick them up!
MARCELLO: Son pezzi di latta?	Are they pieces of tin?

SCHAUNARD: Sei sordo! Sei lippo? Quest'uomo, chi è?

Are you deaf? Are you blind? This man, who's he?

Holds up a coin to Marcello.

RODOLFO: Luigi Philippo! M'inchino al mio re!

Louis Philippe! I bow to my king!

RODOLFO, MARCELLO, COLLINE, SCHAUNARD: Sta Luigi Philippo ai nostri piè!

Louis Philippe is at our feet!

They put the money on the table.

SCHAUNARD: Or vi dirò: quest'oro—o meglio, argento—ha la sua brava storia. . . .

Now I'll tell you: this gold—or rather, silver—has its own gallant history. . . .

The others are busily arranging and preparing the food, and not listening.

MARCELLO: Riscaldiamo il camino!

Let's heat up the stove again!

COLLINE: Tanto freddo ha sofferto!

It's suffered so much from the cold!

SCHAUNARD: Un inglese, un signor, Lord, or milord, che sia, volea un musicista—

An Englishman, a sir, Lord, or milord, whatever it is, wanted a musician—

Marcello pushes Colline's books off the table.

MARCELLO: Via! Prepariamo la tavola!

Off! Let's set the table!

SCHAUNARD: Io? Volo!

Me? I go flying!

RODOLFO: L'esca, dov'è?

The fire materials, where are they?

COLLINE: Là!

There!

MARCELLO: Qua.

Here.

They continue building the fire, lighting the candles, setting the table, and not listening to Schaunard.

SCHAUNARD: E mi presento—m'accetta, gli domando . . .

And, present myself—he receives me, I ask him . . .

COLLINE: Arrosto freddo!

Cold roast beef!

MARCELLO: Pasticcio dolce!

Sweet pastry!

SCHAUNARD:. . . A quando le lezioni? Mi presento, m'accetta, e gli domando: a quando le lezioni? Risponde: "Incominciam!" "Guardare!" e un papagallo m'addita al primo pian, poi soggiunge, "Voi suonare finchè quello morire!"

. . . When are the lessons? I present myself, he receives me, I ask him: when are the lessons? He answers: "We start now." "Look!" And he shows me a parrot on the first floor, and adds, "You're to play until that thing dies!"

RODOLFO: Fulgida folgori la sala splendida.

Let the light brighten the room splendidly.

SCHAUNARD: E fu così: Suonai tre lunghi dì . . .

And so it was: I played for three long days . . .

MARCELLO: Or le candele!

Now the candles!

COLLINE: Pasticcio dolce!

Sweet pastry!

SCHAUNARD: Allora usai l'incanto di mia presenza bella, di mia presenza bella . . .

Then I used the charm of my handsome presence, of my handsome presence . . .

MARCELLO: Mangiar senza tovaglia?

Eating without a tablecloth?

SCHAUNARD: Affascinai l'ancella . . .

I bewitched the servant girl . . .

RODOLFO: Un'idea!

An inspiration!

MARCELLO and COLLINE: Il *Constituzional!*

The *Constitutional!*

They arrange the newspaper as tablecloth.

RODOLFO: Ottima carta! Si mangia e si divora un' appendice!

Excellent paper! One eats and one devours a news supplement!

SCHAUNARD: Gli propinai prezzemolo. Lorito allargò l'ali, Lorito allargò l'ali, Lorito il becco aprì, un poco di prezzemolo, da Socrate morì!	I fed him parsley, Lorito spread his wings, Lorito spread his wings, Lorito opened his beak, a little bit of parsley, like Socrates he died!*
COLLINE: Chi?	Who?

Schaunard stops the others just as they are about to eat.

SCHAUNARD: Che il diavolo vi porti tutti quanti! Ed or che fate? No! Queste ciberie sono la salmeria pei dì futuri tenebrosi e oscuri. Pranzare in casa il dì della vigilia mentre il Quartier Latino le sue vie addobba di salsiccie e leccornie? Quando un'olezzo di frittelle imbalsama le vecchie strade? Là le ragazze cantano contente!	The devil take you all! And now what are you doing? No! This food is insurance for the dark and gloomy future. To eat at home on Christmas Eve, while the Latin Quarter's ways are decorated with sausages and tempting things? While the fragrance of fritters perfumes the old streets? Out there the girls are singing merrily!
RODOLFO, MARCELLO & COLLINE: La vigilia di Natal!	The night before Christmas!
SCHAUNARD: Ed han per eco ognuna uno studente. Un po' di religione, o miei signori: si beva in casa, ma si pranzi fuor!	And every one of them has a student for an echo! A little religion, if you please, gentlemen: let's drink at home, but let's eat out!

As they pour wine, there is a knock on the door.

BENOIT: Si può?	*From without.* May I come in?
MARCELLO: Chi è là?	Who's there?
BENOIT: Benoit.	Benoit.
MARCELLO: Il padrone di casa!	The landlord!

* The belief that parsley is poisonous to parrots sounds like an old wives' tale, but it happens to be true.

SCHAUNARD: Uscio sul muso!	Keep the door shut on his ugly face!
COLLINE: Non c'è nessuno.	There's nobody here.
SCHAUNARD: È chiuso.	It's locked.
BENOIT: Una parola.	Just a word.
SCHAUNARD: Sola!	One!

He opens the door and Benoit enters.

BENOIT: Affitto!	Rent!
MARCELLO: Olà! Date una sedia!	*Very cordially.* Hello! Give him a chair!
RODOLFO: Presto.	Right away.
BENOIT: Non occorre. Vorrei. . . .	Don't trouble. I'd like . . .
SCHAUNARD: Segga.	Sit down.
MARCELLO: Vuol bere?	Want a drink?
BENOIT: Grazie.	Thank you.
RODOLFO: Tocchiamo!	Here's to you!
COLLINE: Tocchiamo!	Here's to you!
SCHAUNARD: Beva!	Drink!
RODOLFO: Tocchiam!	Here's to you!
BENOIT: Quest'è l'ultimo trimestre. . . .	This is the last quarter. . . .

He shows Marcello a piece of paper.

MARCELLO: N'ho piacere.	How nice.
BENOIT: E quindi. . . .	And therefore . . .
SCHAUNARD: Ancora un sorso.	Another sip.
BENOIT: Grazie!	Thank you!
RODOLFO: Tocchiam!	Here's to you!

COLLINE: Tocchiam!	Here's to you!
RODOLFO, MARCELLO, SCHAUNARD & COLLINE: Alla sua salute!	To your health!
BENOIT: A lei ne vengo perchè il trimestre scorso . . . mi promise. . . .	I come to you because last quarter . . . you promised me. . . .
MARCELLO: Promisi ed or mantengo.	I made a promise, and now I'll keep it.
RODOLFO: Che fai?	*Aside to Marcello.* What are you doing?
SCHAUNARD: Sei pazzo?	*Aside to Marcello.* Are you crazy?
MARCELLO: Ha visto? Or via resti un momento in nostra compagnia. Dica: quant'-anni ha, caro Signor Benoit?	See? Now stay a while in our company. Tell us: how old are you, dear Mr. Benoit?
BENOIT: Gl'anni? Per carità!	How old? For pity's sake!

The four see to it that Benoit's glass is never empty.

RODOLFO: Su e giù la nostra età?	More or less our age?
BENOIT: Di più, molto di più.	More, much more.
COLLINE: Ha detto su e giù.	He said more or less.
MARCELLO: L'altra sera, al Mabil, l'han colto in peccato d'amor!	The other night, at Mabille, they caught him in an amorous transgression.
BENOIT: Io?	Me?
MARCELLO: Al Mabil, l'altra sera, l'han colto. Neghi!	At Mabille, the other night, they caught you. Deny it!
BENOIT: Un caso.	A mischance.
MARCELLO: Bella donna!	Lovely lady!

BENOIT: Ah! Molto.	Ah! Very.
SCHAUNARD: Briccone!	Rascal!
RODOLFO: Briccone!	Rascal!
COLLINE: Seduttore!	Seducer!
SCHAUNARD: Briccone!	Rascal!
RODOLFO: Briccone!	Rascal!
MARCELLO: Una quercia! Un cannone.	An oak tree! A cannon!
RODOLFO: L'uomo ha buon gusto.	The man has good taste.
BENOIT: Ha! Ha!	Ha! Ha!
MARCELLO: Il crin ricciuto e fulvo—	Frizzled blonde hair—
SCHAUNARD: Briccon!	Rascal!
MARCELLO: Ei gongolava arzillo, pettorutto—	He was smirking content, strutting about—
BENOIT: Son vecchio, ma robusto.	I'm old but robust.
RODOLFO, SCHAUNARD, & COLLINE: Ei gongolava, arzuto e pettorillo!	*With mock solemnity.* He was exulting, strutting about!
MARCELLO: E a lui cedea la femminil virtù.	And feminine virtue was yielding to him.
BENOIT: Timido in gioventù, ora me ne ripago. Si sa, è uno svago qualche donnetta allegra; e un po'—non dico una balena o un mappamondo, o un visto tondo da luna piena, ma magra, proprio magra, no, poi no.	*Becoming very confidential.* I was bashful in my youth, now I'm making up for it. You know, some gay little lady is a diversion; and a bit—I don't say a whale, or a world globe, or a face as round as the full moon, but lean, downright

Le donne magre son grattacapi e spesso sopraccapi, e son piene di doglie, per esempio mia moglie—	lean, no, then, no. Lean women are headaches and often nuisances, and they're full of troubles, for example my wife—

Marcello rises in great indignation.

MARCELLO: Quest'uomo ha moglie e sconcie voglie ha nel cor!	This man has a wife, and he has these unbecoming lusts in his heart!
SCHAUNARD and COLLINE: Orror!	Horrors!
RODOLFO: E ammorba e appesta la nostra onesta magion!	He both taints and defiles our honest abode!
SCHAUNARD and COLLINE: Fuor!	Out!
MARCELLO: Si abbrucci dello zucchero!	This place must be purified!
COLLINE: Si discacci il reprobo!	The reprobate must be expelled!
SCHAUNARD: È la morale offesa—	It is our injured morality—
BENOIT: Io di . . . Io di . . .	I say . . . I say . . .

He is surrounded and slowly pushed toward the door.

MARCELLO: Silenzio!	Silence!
COLLINE: Silenzio!	Silence!
RODOLFO: Silenzio!	Silence!
SCHAUNARD: —che vi scaccia.	—that expels you.
BENOIT: Miei signori—	Gentlemen—
MARCELLO, SCHAUNARD, and COLLINE: Silenzio! Via, signore!	Silence! Out, sir!

RODOLFO, MARCELLO, SCHAUNARD and COLLINE: Via di qua! E buona sera a vostra signori—Ah! Ah! Ah! Ah!	Away from here! And a good evening to your lordship! Ha! Ha! Ha! Ha!

They return to the center of the room, laughing.

MARCELLO: Ho pagato il trimestre.	I've paid up the quarter.
SCHAUNARD: Al Quartiere Latin ci attende Momus—	Momus awaits us at the Latin Quarter—
MARCELLO: Viva chi spende!	Long live the spendthrift!
SCHAUNARD: Dividiamo il botin.	Let's divide the loot.

They divide the money on the table.

RODOLFO: Dividiam!	Let's divide it!
COLLINE: Dividiam!	Let's divide it!
MARCELLO: Là ci son beltà scese dall cielo. Or che sei ricco, bada alla decenza. Orso, ravviati il pelo.	*To Colline.* Yonder, there are beauties descended straight from the heavens. Now that you're rich, have a care for decency. Bear, get your pelt attended to.
COLLINE: Farò la conoscenza la prima volta d'un barbi tonsore. Guidatemi al ridicolo oltraggio d'un rasoio. Andiam!	I'll make the acquaintance of a barber for the first time. Lead me to the ridiculous outrage of a razor. Let's go!
SCHAUNARD: Andiam, andiam.	Let's go, let's go.
MARCELLO: Andiam.	Let's go.
COLLINE: Andiam.	Let's go.
RODOLFO: Io resto per terminar l'articolo di fondo del *Castoro*.	I'm staying to finish the lead article for *The Beaver*.
MARCELLO: Fa presto.	Make it quick.

Rodolfo escorts the others to the door.

RODOLFO: Cinque minuti. Conosco il mestier.	Five minutes. I know the work.
COLLINE: T'aspetterem dabasso dal portier.	We'll wait for you down at the porter's.
MARCELLO: Se tardi, udrai che coro!	If you're late, what a noise you'll hear!
RODOLFO: Cinque minuti.	Five minutes.
SCHAUNARD: Taglia corto la coda al tuo Castor.	Cut short your Beaver's tale.

Rodolfo returns and sits down at the table; the others' voices are heard from outside.

MARCELLO: Occhio alla scala. Tienti alla ringhiera.	Keep your eyes on the stairs. Hang on to the banister.
RODOLFO: Adagio!	Slow!
COLLINE: È buio pesto.	It's completely dark.
SCHAUNARD: Maledetto portier.	Damn the porter.

There is a loud thump from outside.

COLLINE: Accidenti!	Hell!
RODOLFO: Colline, sei morto?	Colline, are you dead?
COLLINE: Non ancor.	Not yet.
MARCELLO: Vien presto.	Come quick.

Brief musical interlude; Rodolfo throws down his pen.

RODOLFO: Non sono in vena.	I'm not in the mood.

There is a knock on the door.

Chi è là?	Who's there?
MIMI: Scusi.	*From outside.* Excuse me.
RODOLFO: Una donna!	A lady!
MIMI: Di grazia, mi s'è spento il lume.	Please, my candle has gone out.

Rodolfo opens the door.

RODOLFO: Ecco.	There.
MIMI: Vorrebbe. . . . ?	Would you . . . ?
RODOLFO: S'accomodi un momento.	Sit down for a moment.
MIMI: Non occorre.	It isn't necessary.
RODOLFO: La prego, entri.	I pray you, come in.

Mimi coughs.

Si sente male?	Do you feel sick?
MIMI: No—nulla.	No—it's nothing.
RODOLFO: Impallidisce.	You are turning pale.

Mimi almost faints; Rodolfo barely catches her and helps her to a chair; she drops her key and her candlestick.

MIMI: Il respir—quelle scale—	My breath—those stairs—

Rodolfo fetches some water and sprinkles it on Mimi's face.

RODOLFO: Ed ora, come faccio? Così. Che viso d'ammalata! Si sente meglio?	And now, what can I do? There. What a pale face! Do you feel better?
MIMI: Sì.	Yes.
RODOLFO: Qui c'è tanto freddo. Segga vicino al fuoco—Aspetti—un po' di vino—	It's so cold here. Sit near the fire—Wait—a bit of wine—
MIMI: Grazie.	Thank you.

Rodolfo pours some wine.

RODOLFO: A lei.	To you.
MIMI: Poco, poco.	A little bit, a little bit.
RODOLFO: Così?	Like this?
MIMI: Grazie.	Thank you.

RODOLFO: (Che bella bambina!)	(What a beautiful little girl!)
MIMI: Ora permette che accenda il lume. È tutto passato.	Now allow me to light the candle. It's all passed.
RODOLFO: Tanta fretta?	So fast?

He picks up the candlestick and hands it to her.

MIMI: Sì. Grazie. Buona sera.	Yes. Thank you. Good evening.

She starts to leave.

RODOLFO: Buona sera.	Good evening.

Mimi stops on the threshold.

MIMI: Oh! Sventata, sventata! La chiave della stanza, dove l'ho lasciata?	Oh, scatterbrain, scatterbrain! The key to my room, where have I left it?
RODOLFO: Non stia sull'uscio; il lume vacilla al vento.	Don't stand in the doorway; your candle is flickering in the wind.

Mimi's light goes out.

MIMI: Oh, Dio! Torni ad accenderlo.	Oh, Lord! Would you come light it again?

Rodolfo approaches with a candle, but it goes out too.

RODOLFO: Oh, Dio! Anche il mio s'è spento!	Oh, Lord! Mine's gone out too.
MIMI: Ah! E la chiave, ove sarà?	Ah! And where can the key be?

She gropes her way back to the table and sets down the candlestick.

RODOLFO: Buio pesto!	Completely dark!
MIMI: Disgraziata!	I'm so sorry!
RODOLFO: Ove sarà?	Where can it be?
MIMI: Importuna è la vicina...	Your neighbor is troublesome . . .
RODOLFO: Ma le pare!	Don't mention it!

They both grope on the floor for the key.

MIMI: Importuna è la vicina. . .	Your neighbor is troublesome. . . .
RODOLFO: Cosa dice, ma le pare.	What are you saying, don't mention it.
MIMI: Cerchi?	Would you look?
RODOLFO: Cerco.	I am looking.
MIMI: Ove sarà?	Where can it be?
RODOLFO: Ah!	Ah!

Rodolfo finds the key and furtively slips it into his pocket.

MIMI: L'ha trovata?	Have you found it?
RODOLFO: No.	No.
MIMI: Mi parve. . . .	I thought . . .
RODOLFO: In verità.	Honestly.
MIMI: Cerca?	Are you looking?
RODOLFO: Cerco!	I'm looking!

Pretends to continue searching, and gropes his way nearer to Mimi; finally he manages to touch her hand in the darkness.

MIMI: Ah!	Ah!

Surprised, she stands up.

RODOLFO: Che gelida manina, se la lasci riscaldar. Cercar che giova? Al buio non si trova. Ma per fortuna, è una notta di luna . . . e qui la luna, l'abbiamo vicina. Aspetti, signorina, le dirò con due parole chi son, chi son, e che faccio, come vivo. Vuole? Chi son? Chi son? Sono un poeta. Che cosa faccio? Scrivo. E come vivo? Vivo.	What a frozen little hand, would you let me warm it? What's the good of searching? We won't find it in the dark. But by luck it is a moonlit night, and we'll have the moon near us here. Wait, miss, and I'll tell you in a couple of words who I am—who I am, and what I do, how I live. Would you like that? Who am I? Who am I? I'm a poet. What do I do? I

In povertà mia lieta scialo da gran signore rime ed inni d'amore. Per sogni e per chimere e per castelli in aria l'anima ho millionaria. Talor dal mio forziere ruban tutti i gioielli due ladri: gli occhi belli. V'entrar con voi pur ora, ed i miei sogni usati, e i bei sogni miei tosto si dileguar! Ma il furto non m'accora poichè—poichè v'ha preso stanza la dolce speranza! Or che mi conoscete, parlate voi, deh! Parlate! Che siete? Vi piaccia dir!

write. And how do I live? I live. In my poverty I feast as gaily as a grand lord on rhymes and hymns of love. For dreams and fancies and castles in the air, I have a millionaire's soul. Now and then two thieves rob all the jewels from my strongbox: two beautiful eyes. They came in with you, just now, and my old dreams, my beautiful dreams, quickly dissolved. But the theft doesn't hurt me, since—since such sweet expectation has taken its stead. Now that you know me, come, you speak. Who are you? Please tell!

Rodolfo releases Mimi's hand, and she drops into a chair.

MIMI: Sì. Mi chiamano Mimì, ma il mio nome è Lucia. La storia mia è breve. A tela o a seta ricamo in casa e fuori. Son tranquilla e lieta ed è mio svago far giglie e rose—Mi piaccion quelle cose che han sì dolce malia, che parlano d'amor, di primavere, che parlano di sogni e di chimere—quelle cose che han nome poesia—Lei m'intende?

Yes. They call me Mimi, but my name is Lucia. My story is brief. I embroider silk or linen at home and outside. I'm contented and happy, and it's my pleasure to make lilies and roses. I like those things that have sweet charm, that speak of love, of springtimes, that speak of dreams and fancies—those things that are called poetry. Do you understand me?

RODOLFO: Sì.

Yes.

MIMI: Mi chiamano Mimì, il perchè non so. Sola, mi fo il pranzo da me stessa. Non

They call me Mimi, but I don't know why. All alone, I make dinner for myself. I

vado sempre a messa ma prego assai il Signor. Vivo sola, soletta, là in una bianca cameretta: guardo sui tetti e in cielo, ma quando vien lo sgelo il primo sole è mio—il primo bacio dell'aprile è mio! Il primo sole è mio! Germoglia in un vaso una rosa. Foglia a foglia la spiro! Così gentil il profumo d'un fior! Ma i fior ch'io faccio, ahimè, i fior ch'io faccio, ahimè, non hanno odore! Altro di me non le saprei narrare: sono la sua vicina che la vien fuori d'ora a importunare.	don't always go to Mass, but I often pray to the Lord. I live alone, all by myself, in a little white room over there. I look on the roofs and into the sky, but when the thaw comes, the first sunshine is mine—the first kiss of April is mine. The first sunshine is mine! A rose opens in a vase. Leaf by leaf I sniff its fragrance. So lovely is the perfume of a flower. But the flowers that I make—alas! the flowers that I make—alas! have no odor. I wouldn't know anything else to tell you about myself—I'm your neighbor who comes at this odd hour to trouble you.

Voices are heard from outside.

SCHAUNARD: Ehi! Rodolfo!	Hey! Rodolfo!
COLLINE: Rodolfo!	Rodolfo!
MARCELLO: Olà! Non senti? Lumaca!	Hey there! Don't you hear? Snail!
COLLINE: Poetucolo!	Paltry little rhymester!
SCHAUNARD: Accidenti al pigro!	Confound the slowpoke!

Rodolfo goes to the window and calls down.

RODOLFO: Scrivo ancor tre righe a volo.	I still have three lines to write in a flash.

Mimi comes to the window beside Rodolfo.

MIMI: Chi son?	Who are they?
RODOLFO: Amici.	*To Mimi.* Friends.
SCHAUNARD: Sentirai le tue!	You'll get yours!

MARCELLO: Che te ne fai lì solo?	What are you doing up there all alone?
RODOLFO: Non son solo. Siamo in due. Andate a Momus, tenete il posto, ci saremo tosto.	I'm not alone. There are two of us. Go to Momus, hold a place, we'll be there soon.
MARCELLO, SCHAUNARD and COLLINE: Momus, Momus, Momus, zitti e discreti, andiamocene, via!	Momus, Momus, Momus, quiet and discreet, let's get away from here, away!
SCHAUNARD and COLLINE: Momus, Momus!	Momus, Momus!
MARCELLO: Trovò la poesia!	He found poetry!

Their voices fade into the distance.

SCHAUNARD and COLLINE: Momus, Momus, Momus!	Momus, Momus, Momus!

A moonbeam shines through the window on Mimi, Rodolfo, turning, sees her.

RODOLFO: O soave fanciulla—	O gentle girl—
MARCELLO: Trovò la poesia!	*From far away.* He found poetry!
RODOLFO: O dolce viso di mite circonfuso alba lunar, in te ravviso il sogno ch'io vorrei sempre sognar.	O sweet face surrounded by mild white moonlight, the dream I would always dream comes to life in you.

The following is a duet.

MIMI: Ah! tu sol commandi, amor!	Ah! love, you alone may rule!
RODOLFO: Fremon già nell'anima—le dolcezze estreme—	Already extreme joys are thrilling in my soul—
MIMI: Tu sol commandi, amore!	Love, you alone may rule!
RODOLFO: Fremon nell' anima—	Are thrilling in my soul—

MIMI: Oh! Come dolci scendono le sue lusinghe al core, tu sol commandi, amor!	Oh! How sweetly your soft words sink into my heart, love, you alone may rule!
RODOLFO: —dolcezze estreme —fremon dolcezze estreme, nel bacio freme amor.	—extreme joys—extreme joys are thrilling, love thrills in the kiss.

He kisses Mimi.

MIMI: No, per pietà!	No, please!

She frees herself.

RODOLFO: Sei mia!	You're mine!
MIMI: V'aspettan gli amici.	Your friends are waiting for you.
RODOLFO: Già mi mandi via?	You send me away already?
MIMI: Vorrei dir, ma non oso—	I'd like to ask, but I don't dare—
RODOLFO: Dì!	Ask it!
MIMI: Se venissi con voi?	If I could come with you?
RODOLFO: Che? Mimi! Sarebbe così dolce restar qui. C'è freddo fuori—	What? Mimi! It would be so pleasant to stay here. It's cold outside—
MIMI: Vi starò vicina.	I'll stay near you.
RODOLFO: E al ritorno?	And on returning?
MIMI: Curioso!	*Coquettishly.* Inquisitive!
RODOLFO: Dammi il braccio, mia piccina.	*Gallantly.* Take my arm, my little one.
MIMI: Obbedisco, signor!	I obey, sir!

They exit, arm in arm; remainder of duet is heard from outside.

RODOLFO: Che m'ami, dì!	Say that you love me!
MIMI: Io t'amo.	I love you.
RODOLFO and MIMI: Amor! Amor! Amor!	Love! Love! Love!

(Courtesy Royal Opera House, Covent Garden, London. Photo by Roger Wood)

Act. 1. Rodolfo burns his manuscript to heat the garret.

(Courtesy Museum of the Bolshoi Theater, Moscow)

Act. 1. The Bohemians dine in their garret. From a 1956 performance.

ACT TWO

(Courtesy Berlin Civic Opera. Photo by Scherl Studios)

Setting for Act 2. The influence of Brecht is visible in this production.

ACT TWO

Time: Later that same evening.

Scene: A square surrounded by gaily decorated shops. One side, sign "Café Momus," with tables and chairs. A large motley crowd of students, shopgirls, vendors, sightseers, and street arabs mills about. Hawkers proclaim their wares; excited street arabs follow them, mimicking their shouts.

As the curtain rises, SCHAUNARD is buying a tin horn from a vendor; COLLINE bargains with a ragshop proprietor. RODOLFO and MIMI approach arm in arm, remaining a little aloof from the crowd and engrossed in each other. MARCELLO is hustled about by the crowd.

A brief, gay, brassy orchestral prelude begins the act.

More or less all at the same time

HAWKERS: Aranci, datteri, caldi i marroni! Ninnoli, croci, torroni!	Oranges, dates, hot chestnuts! Trinkets, crosses. Almond cakes!
SOPRANOS: Ah! Ah!	Ah! Ah!
TENORS: Quanta folla! Che chiasso!	Such a mob! What an uproar!
STREET ARABS: Aranci, ninnoli! Caldi i marroni e caramelle! Torroni!	Oranges, trinkets! Hot chestnuts and caramels! Almond cakes!
HAWKERS: Panna montata! Caramelle! La crostata!	Whipped cream! Caramels! Tarts!
HAWKERS: Oh! La crostata! Fiori alle belle! Panna montata!	Oh! Tarts! Flowers for the lovely ladies! Whipped cream!
SOPRANOS: Quanto folla! Stringiti a me, che chiasso!	Such a mob! Hold tight to me, what an uproar!

More or less all at the same time

TENORS: Su, corriam! Stringiti a me. Su, corriam!	Come on, let's hurry! Hold tight to me. Come on, let's hurry!
STREET ARABS: Su, corriamo, su corriam!	Come on, let's hurry, come on, let's hurry!
HAWKERS: Fringuelli, passeri! Caldi i marroni! Panna, torroni!	Chaffinches, sparrows! Hot chestnuts! Cream, almond cakes!
HAWKERS: Datteri! Latte di cocco! Oh! La crostata!	Dates! Coconut milk! Oh! Tarts!
SOPRANOS: Date il passo, corriam!	Let us through, let's hurry!
TENORS: Date il passo, corriam!	Let us through, let's hurry!
STREET ARABS: Datteri, aranci! Latte di cocco!	Dates, oranges! Coconut milk!
SOPRANOS & TENORS: Quanta folla! Su, partiam!	Such a mob! Come on, let's leave!
STREET ARABS: Caldi i marroni! Ninnoli, torroni!	Hot chestnuts! Trinkets, almond cakes!
HAWKERS: Panna montata, ninnoli, torroni!	Whipped cream, trinkets, almond cakes!
HAWKERS: Aranci, fiori, datteri, torroni!	Oranges, flowers, dates, almond cakes!
SOPRANOS: Ah! Date il passo!	Ah! Let us through!

To waiters milling about Café.

TENORS: Ah! Presto qua!	Ah! Here, quick!
BASSO: Camerier!	Waiter!
TENORS: Un bicchier! Corri! Da ber!	A glass! Hurry! Something to drink!
SOPRANOS: Ah! Quanta folla!	Ah! Such a crowd!
BASSO: Birra!	Beer!

More or less all at the same time

SOPRANOS & TENORS: Stringiti a me, corriam!	Hold tight to me, let's hurry!
STREET ARABS: Fringuelli e passeri! Caldi i marron!	Chaffinches and sparrows! Hot chestnuts!
SOMEONE YELLING: Emma! Quando ti chiamo!	Emma! When I'm calling you!
BASSO: Dunque! Un caffè!	Now then! Coffee!
TENOR: Da ber!	Something to drink!
STREET ARABS: Voglio una lancia! Aranci, caldi i marron!	I want a spear! Oranges, hot chestnuts!
BASSO: Camerier!	Waiter!
TENOR: Olà!	Hey there!
SOPRANOS: Che chiasso! Stringiti a me!	What an uproar! Hold tight to me!
HAWKERS: Latte di cocco! Giubbe! Carote!	Coconut milk! Waistcoats! Carrots!
TENORS: Quanta folla, su, partiam!	Such a mob, come on, let's leave!
STREET ARABS: Datteri! Ninnoli, aranci e fior!	Dates! Trinkets, oranges and flowers!

Some of the hawkers and street arabs begin to move away; the crowd thins slightly. Schaunard, having bargained for and bought his horn, blows it vigorously.

SCHAUNARD: Falso questo Re! Falso questo Re! Pipa e corno, quant'è?	This "re" is off! This "re" is off! How much for the pipe and the horn?

Mimi and Rodolfo make their way through the mob to a milliner's. Colline speaks to the ragshop owner who has mended his coat.

COLLINE: È un poco usato—	It's a bit worn—
RODOLFO: Andiam.	Let's go.

MIMI: Andiam per la cuffietta?	Are we going for the bonnet?
COLLINE: —ma è serio e a buon mercato.	—but it's sturdy, and at a good price.

He puts on the coat, filling its innumerable capacious pockets with books.

RODOLFO: Tienti al mio braccio stretta—	Hold tight to my arm—
MIMI: A te mi stringo.	I'm holding on to you.
RODOLFO & MIMI: Andiam!	Let's go.

They enter the milliner's. Marcello, carrying a package, eyes various girls in the crowd with great interest.

MARCELLO: Io pur mi sento in vena di gridar: Chi vuol, donnine allegre, un po' d'amor?	I feel in the mood for shouting, too: Pretty little girls, who wants a bit of love?
HAWKER: Datteri!	Dates!
HAWKER: Trote!	Trout!
HAWKER: Prugne di Tours!	Prunes from Tours!
MARCELLO: Facciamo insieme—facciamo a vendere e a comprar!	*To a girl in the crowd.* Let's play together—let's play buying and selling!
HAWKER: Prugne di Tours!	Prunes from Tours!
MARCELLO: Io dò un soldo il vergine mio cuor!	For one cent I'll give away my virgin heart!

The girl laughs and disappears in the crowd.

SCHAUNARD: Fra spintoni e pestate accorrendo affretta la folla e si diletta nel provar gioie matte insoddisfatte.*	The frantic mob rushes back and forth between jostling and lurching, and delights in experiencing its crazy, insatiable pleasures.

* Readers of the original libretto will also find the words: "Se la spassa così con poche spese il buon ceto borghese." ("The good middle class amuses itself thus with little expense.") Puccini made this change, as well as a few others in Act Two, after the first performance of *La Bohème*.

He wanders about with his horn and a huge pipe, and watches the crowd.

2 WOMEN HAWKERS: Ninnoli, spillette! Datteri e caramelle!	Trinkets, pins! Dates and caramels!
HAWKERS: Fiori alle belle!	Flowers for the lovely ladies!
STREET ARABS: Ah!—	Ah!—

Colline approaches, happily waving an old book.

COLLINE: Copia rara, anzi unica; la grammatica runica!	Rare copy, quite unique; a Runic grammar!
SCHAUNARD: Uomo onesto!	Honest man!
MARCELLO: A cena!	*Calling from Café.* To supper!
SCHAUNARD & COLLINE: Rodolfo?	Rodolfo?
MARCELLO: Entrò da una modista.	He went into a milliner's.
RODOLFO: Vieni, gli amici aspettano.	Come on, my friends are waiting.
HAWKERS: Panna montata!	Whipped cream!

Marcello, Schaunard and Colline look for an empty table. Not finding one, they glare at the occupants of one particular table and enter the Café.

MIMI: Mi sta ben questa cuffietta rosa?	Does this pink bonnet look well on me?
STREET ARABS: Latte di cocco!	Coconut milk!
HAWKER: Oh! La crostata!	Oh! Tarts!
HAWKER: Panna montata!	Whipped cream!
TENOR: Camerier!	Waiter!
RODOLFO: Sei bruna e quel color ti dona.	You're brunette and that color suits you.
BASSO: Un bicchier!	A glass!

TENOR: Presto, olà!	*From inside the Café.* Hurry, hey, there!
BASSO: Ratafìa!	Cherry liqueur!
MIMI: Bel vezzo di corallo!	Pretty coral necklace!
RODOLFO: Ho uno zio millionario. Se fa senno il buon Dio, voglio comprarti un vezzo assai più bel!	I have a millionaire uncle. If the good Lord decides, I'll want to buy you a much prettier necklace.

They continue talking and are swallowed by the crowd; a vendor, standing on a chair or table in the rear, offers lingerie and nightgowns for sale. The girls around him laugh.

More or less all at the same time

STREET ARABS: Ah! Ah! Ah! Ah! Ah! Ah! Ah! Ah! Ah! Ah!	Ha! Ha! Ha! Ha! Ha! Ha! Ha! Ha! Ha! Ha!
GIRLS & STUDENTS: Ah! Ah!	Ha! Ha!
STREET ARABS, GIRLS & STUDENTS: Ah! Ah! Ah! Ah! Ah! Ah! Ah! Ah! Ah!	Ha! Ha! Ha! Ha! Ha! Ha! Ha! Ha! Ha!
CITIZENS: Facciam coda a la gente.	Let's follow the people.
HAWKER: Oh, la crostata!	Oh tarts!
TENOR: Ragazze, state attente!	Girls, look out!
SOPRANO: Che chiasso! Quanta folla!	What an uproar! Such a mob!
STREET ARABS: Oh, la crostata!	Oh tarts!
HAWKER: Panna montata!	Whipped cream!
TENOR: Pigliam Via Mazzarino!	Let's take Mazarin Street!
STREET ARABS: Panna montata!	Whipped cream!

SOPRANO: Io soffoco, partiamo!	I'm stifling, let's leave!
HAWKER: Fiori alle belle!	Flowers for the lovely ladies!
TENOR: Vedi! Il caffè è vicin!	See? The coffee is at hand!
SOPRANO & TENOR: Andiam là da Momus!	Let's go there from Momus.
STREET ARABS: Ninnoli, datteri, caldi marron!	Trinkets, dates, hot chestnuts!
HAWKER: Aranci, datteri, ninnoli, fior!	Oranges, dates, trinkets, flowers!
HAWKER: Fringuelli, passeri, panna, torron!	Chaffinches, sparrows, cream, almond cakes!
TENOR & SOPRANO: Ah!	Ah!

Marcello, Colline and Schaunard emerge from the Café carrying a table; they are followed by a waiter with chairs. People at the next table move on. Rodolfo and Mimi reappear.

RODOLFO: Che guardi?	What are you looking at?
COLLINE: Odio il profano volgo al par d'Orazio.	As did Horace, I hate the vulgar mob.
MIMI: Sei geloso?	Are you jealous?
RODOLFO: All'uom felice sta il sospetto accanto.	Suspicion stands beside the happy man.
SCHAUNARD: Ed io, quando mi sazio, vo' abbondanza di spazio.	And I, when I fill myself, want plenty of space.
MIMI: Sei felice?	Are you happy?
MARCELLO: Vogliamo una cena prelibata.	*To a waiter.* We want an excellent supper.
RODOLFO: Ah! Sì, tanto! E tu?	Ah! Yes, very much! And you?
MARCELLO: Lesto!	Quickly!

SCHAUNARD: Per molti.	For several.
MIMI: Sì, tanto.	Yes, very much.
TENOR: Là da Momus.	There from Momus.
1st SOPRANO: Andiam!	Let's go!
2nd SOPRANO: Andiam!	Let's go!
MARCELLO, COLLINE & SCHAUNARD: Lesto!	*To the waiter setting the table.* Quickly!

Parpignol is heard from the distance.

PARPIGNOL: Ecco i giocattoli di Parpignol!	Here are the toys of Parpignol!

Rodolfo and Mimi arrive; Rodolfo presents Mimi.

RODOLFO: Due posti.	Two places.
COLLINE: Finalmente!	Finally!
RODOLFO: Eccoci qui. Questa è Mimi, gaia fioraia. Il suo venir completa la bella compagnia — perchè — perchè son io il poetà, essa la poesia. Dal mio cervel sbocciano i canti, dalle sue dita sbocciano i fior—dall' anime esultanti sboccia l'amor, sboccia l'amor!	Here we are. This is Mimi, gay flower girl. Her coming completes this fine company—because—because I am a poet, she is poetry. Songs flow from my brain, flowers bloom from her fingers—from our rejoicing souls love flows, love flows.
MARCELLO, SCHAUNARD & COLLINE: Ah! Ah! Ah! Ah!	Ha! Ha! Ha! Ha!
MARCELLO: Dio, che concetti rari!	*With light irony.* Lord, what exquisite imagery!
COLLINE: *Digna est intrari.*	*Bowing to Mimi. Digna est intrari.*
SCHAUNARD: *Ingrediat si necessit.*	*Gravely. Ingrediat si necessit.*

The waiter returns, and all sit down.

COLLINE: Io non dò che un *accessit*!	I'll only add an *accessit*!

Parpignol draws nearer.

PARPIGNOL: Ecco i giocattoli di Parpignol!	Here are the toys of Parpignol!
COLLINE: Salame!	*Shouting to waiter.* Idiot!

Enter Parpignol, pushing a gaily decorated barrow of toys. Children prance around him. The friends scrutinize the menu.

CHILDREN: Parpignol, Parpignol, Parpignol! Ecco Parpignol, Parpignol, Parpignol! Col carretto tutto fior! Ecco Parpignol, Parpignol, Parpignol, Parpignol!	Parpignol, Parpignol, Parpignol, Parpignol! There's Parpignol, Parpignol, Parpignol! With his cart all flower-covered! There's Parpignol, Parpignol, Parpignol!
1st CHILDREN: Voglio la tromba, il cavallin—	I want the trumpet, the little horse—
2nd CHILDREN: Il tambur, tamburel—	The drum, the little drum—
1st CHILDREN: Voglio il cannon, voglio il frustin—	I want the cannon, I want the whip—
2nd CHILDREN: —dei soldati il drappel.	—the brigade of soldiers.

Scolding mothers approach, but the children won't leave Parpignol.

SCHAUNARD: Cervo arrosto!	*Loudly to waiter.* Roast venison!
MARCELLO: Un tacchino!	Turkey!
SCHAUNARD: Vin del Rheno!	Rhine wine!
COLLINE: Vin da tavola!	Table wine!
SCHAUNARD: Aragosta senza crosta!	Lobster out of the shell!
MOTHERS: Ah! razza di furfanti indemoniati, che ci venite a fare in questo loco? A casa, a letto! Via, brutti sguaiati, gli scappellotti vi parranno poco! A casa, a	*Pursuing children.* Ah! race of demoniac rogues, why did you come here? Home, to bed! Off, ugly stupids, some boxes on your ears may show you a thing or two! Home to

letto, razza di furfanti, a letto!	bed, race of rogues, to bed!
LITTLE BOY: Vo' la tromba, il cavallin!	I want the trumpet, the little horse!
RODOLFO: E tu, Mimi, che vuoi?	And you, Mimi, what do you want?
MIMI: La crema.	Custard.
SCHAUNARD: È gran sfarzo; c'è una dama!	*To waiter.* It's a great occasion; this is a lady!

The mothers relent and buy the toys. The children are delighted. Parpignol moves on.

CHILDREN: Viva Parpignol, Parpignol, Parpignol, Parpignol! Il tambur, tamburel, dei soldati il drappel!	Long live Parpignol, Parpignol, Parpignol, Parpignol! The drum, the little drum, the brigade of soldiers!

Their voices fade off into the distance.

MARCELLO: Signorina Mimi, che dono raro le ha fatto il suo Rodolfo?	Miss Mimi, what rare present has your Rodolfo given to you?
MIMI: Una cuffietta a pizzi, tutta rosa, ricamata; coi miei capelli bruni ben si fonde. Da tanto tempo tal cuffietta è cosa desiata—ed egli ha letto quel che il core asconde—ora colui che legge dentro a un cuore sa l'amore—ed è lettore.	A bonnet with ribbons, all pink, embroidered; it goes well with my brown hair. It has been a thing I've wanted for such a long time—and he has read what the heart conceals—now one who reads into the heart understands love—and is a wise man.
SCHAUNARD: Esperto professore.	Expert professor.
COLLINE: Che ha già diplomi e non son armi prime le sue rime.	Who already has diplomas, and these poems are not his first campaign.
SCHAUNARD: Tanto che	So much so that what he

sembra ver—ciò ch'egli esprime. | expresses appears to be the truth.

MARCELLO: O bella età d'inganni e d'utopie! si crede, spera, e tutto bello appare.

O lovely age of deceptions and utopias! We believe, we hope, and everything seems lovely.

RODOLFO: La più divina delle poesie è quella, amico, che c'insegna amare.

The most divine of poems is the one, friend, which teaches us to love.

MIMI: Amare è dolce ancora più del miele, più del miele!

To love is still sweeter than honey, sweeter than honey!

MARCELLO: Secondo il palato è miele o fiele.

It's honey or gall, according to one's palate.

MIMI: O Dio! L'ho offeso!

Oh Lord! I've offended him!

RODOLFO: È in lutto, o mia Mimi.

He's in mourning, o my Mimi.

SCHAUNARD & COLLINE: Allegri, un toast!

Let's be merry, a toast!

MARCELLO: Qua del liquor!

Bring some wine!

MIMI, RODOLFO & MARCELLO: E via i pensier, alti i bicchier! Beviam!

And away with worries, up with the glasses! Let's drink!

MIMI, RODOLFO, MARCELLO, SCHAUNARD & COLLINE: Beviam!

Let's drink!

MARCELLO: Ch'io beva del tossico!

Let me drink some poison!

Enter Musetta, beautiful and coquettish, followed by the elderly, fussy, and perspiring Alcindoro.

RODOLFO, SCHAUNARD & COLLINE: Oh!

Vastly surprised. Oh!

MARCELLO: Essa!

She!

RODOLFO, SCHAUNARD & COLLINE: Musetta!	Musetta!
SHOPWOMEN: To'!	My!
SHOPWOMEN: Lei!	Her!
SHOPWOMEN: Sì!	Yes!
SHOPWOMEN: To'!	My!
SHOPWOMEN: Lei! Musetta!	Her! Musetta!
SHOPWOMEN: Tornata!	She's come back!
SHOPWOMEN: Siamo in auge!	We've reached the top!
SHOPWOMEN: Che toeletta!	What elegance!
ALCINDORO: Come un facchino correr di qua—di là —no, no! non ci stà!	*Breathless with exertion.* Running hither and yon like a porter—no! no! impossible!
MUSETTA: Vien, Lulù!	*Looks about, as if searching for someone.* Come, Lulu!
ALCINDORO: Non ne posso più!	I can't take any more!

Musetta motions Alcindoro to the recently-vacated table near the friends.

MUSETTA: Vien, Lulù!	Come, Lulu!
ALCINDORO: Non ne posso più!	I can't take any more!
SCHAUNARD: Quel brutto coso, mi pare che sudi!	That ugly what's-his-name, I think he's sweating!
ALCINDORO: Come! Qui fuori? Qui?	What! Out here? Here!
MUSETTA: Siedi, Lulù.	Sit down, Lulu.

Alcindoro obeys, irritatedly.

ALCINDORO: Tali nomignoli, prego serbateli al tu per tu!	Such little names, I pray you, save them for when we are alone!

Waiter begins to set their table.

MUSETTA: Non farmi il Barbablù!	Don't play Bluebeard with me!

COLLINE: È il vizio contegnoso.

Examining Alcindoro. He's a dignified sinner.

MARCELLO: Colla casta Susanna!

With heavy sarcasm. With the chaste Susanna.

MIMI: È pur ben vestita.

To Rodolfo. She's certainly well dressed.

RODOLFO: Gli angeli vanno nudi.

It's the angels who go nude.

MIMI: La conosci? Chi è?

To Rodolfo. Do you know her?

MARCELLO: Domandatelo a me. Il suo nome è Musetta—

Who is she? Ask it of me. Her name is Musetta—

MUSETTA: Marcello mi vide—e non mi guarda, il vile!

Aside. Marcello sees me—and won't look at me, the villain!

MARCELLO: —Cognome: Tentazione! Per sua vocazione fa la rosa dei venti; gira e muta soventi d'amanti e d'amore—

—Surname: Temptation! Her profession is to be a weather vane in the breeze; she changes and alters her love and her lovers often—

Musetta gradually begins to get angry and angrier.

MUSETTA: Quel Schaunard che ride—Mi fan tutti una bile!

Aside. That Schaunard who's laughing—They all make me furious!

MARCELLO: E come la civetta—

And like the screechowl—

MUSETTA: (Se potessi picchiar! Se potessi graffiar!)

(If I could hit him! If I could scratch him!)

MARCELLO: —È uccello sanguinario; il suo cibo ordinario è il cuore.

—She is a bloodthirsty bird; her standard fare is the heart.

MUSETTA: (Ma non ho sotto man che questo pellican.)

(But I haven't any support except this old duck.)

MARCELLO: —Mangia il cuore!	—She eats hearts!
MUSETTA: Aspetta!	Wait!
MARCELLO: Per questo io non ne ho più.	Therefore I no longer have one.
MUSETTA: Ehi! Camerier!	*Yelling.* Hey! Waiter!
MARCELLO: Passatemi il ragù.	Pass me the ragout.

Musetta points to her plate as the waiter comes.

MUSETTA: Ehi! Camerier! Questo piatto ha un puzza di rifritto!	Hey! Waiter! This plate stinks of old fried things!

She smashes the plate on the ground.

ALCINDORO: No. Musetta—zitto, zitto.	No. Musetta—quiet, quiet.
MUSETTA: (Non si volta.)	(He won't turn around.)
ALCINDORO: Zitto! Zitto! Zitto! Modi, garbo!	Quiet! Quiet! Quiet! Manners, nice manners!
MUSETTA: (Ah! non si volta!)	(Ah! he won't turn around!)
ALCINDORO: A chi parli?	To whom are you speaking?
COLLINE: Questo pollo è un poema!	This chicken is a poem!
MUSETTA: (Ora lo batto, lo batto!)	(Now I'll beat him, I'll beat him!)
ALCINDORO: Con chi parli?	To whom are you speaking?
MUSETTA: Al cameriere! Non seccar!	To the waiter. Don't bother me!
SCHAUNARD: Il vino è prelibato.	The wine is excellent.
MUSETTA: Voglio fare il mio piacere—	I will do what I like—

ALCINDORO: Parla pian—	Speak softly—
MUSETTA: Vo' far quel che mi pare!	I will do whatever suits me!

Alcindoro glares over the menu.

ALCINDORO: Parla pian, parla pian!	Speak softly, speak softly!
MUSETTA: Non seccar!	Don't bother me!

Workgirls stare at Musetta as they go by.

WORKGIRLS: Guarda, guarda chi se vede, proprio lei, Musetta!	Look, look who's here, she herself, Musetta!

Students stare at Musetta as they go by.

STUDENTS: Con quel vecchio che balbetta, proprio lei, Musetta!	With that stammering old fool, she herself, Musetta!
WORKGIRLS & STUDENTS: Ah! Ah! Ah! Ah! Ah! Ah! Ah!	Ha! Ha! Ha! Ha! Ha! Ha! Ha!
MUSETTA: (Che sia gelosa di questa mummia?)	(Could he be jealous of this mummy?)

Alcindoro tries to soothe the irate Musetta.

ALCINDORO: La convenienza—	Prudence—
MUSETTA: (Vediam—se mi resta tanto poter su lui da farlo cedere!)	(We'll see—if I still have enough power over him to make him yield!)
ALCINDORO: Il grado—la virtu.—	Dignity—virtue.—
SCHAUNARD: La commedia è stupenda!	The comedy is stupendous!
MUSETTA: Tu non mi guardi!	*Directly to Marcello.* You won't look at me!
ALCINDORO: Vedi bene che ordino!	Look, dear, I'm ordering!

SCHAUNARD: La commedia è stupenda! — The comedy is stupendous!

COLLINE: Stupenda! — Stupendous!

RODOLFO: Sappi per tuo governo che non darei perdono in sempiterno. — *To Mimi.* Remember for your own good that I would never forgive you.

SCHAUNARD: Essa all'un parla perchè l'altro intenda. — She speaks to one so that the other understands.

MIMI: Io t'amo tanto, e sono tutta tua! — *To Rodolfo.* I love you so much, and I'm all yours!

COLLINE: E l'altro invan crudel— — *To Schaunard.* And the other, vainly cruel—

MIMI: Che mi parli di perdono? — What are you saying to me about forgiveness?

COLLINE: —finge di non capir, ma sugge miel! — —pretends not to understand, but is delighted!

MUSETTA: Ma il tuo cuore martella— — But your heart is pounding—

ALCINDORO: Parla piano— — Speak softly—

MUSETTA: Ma il tuo cuore martella— — But your heart is pounding—

ALCINDORO: —piano, piano! — —softly, softly!

Musetta still sits, but very obviously sings to Marcello.

MUSETTA: Quando me'n vo'—quando me'n vo' soletta per la via, la gente sosta e mira, e la bellezza mia tutta ricerca in me, ricerca in me, da capo a piè— — Whenever I walk—whenever I walk alone through the streets, the people stop and stare, and everybody looks at my beauty, looks at me, from head to foot—

MARCELLO: Legatemi alla seggiola! — *Most agitatedly.* Tie me to the chair!

ALCINDORO: Quella gente, che dirà? — Those people, what will they say?

MUSETTA: —ed assaporo allor la bramosia sottil—che da gl'occhi traspira e dai palesi vezzi intender sa—alle occulte beltà. Così l'effluvio del desio tutta m'aggira felice mi fa, felice mi fa.	—and then I sense the sharp desire—that escapes from their eyes, and that their open endearments make clear—for my hidden beauties. Such an outpouring of longing whirls me about, makes me completely happy, makes me happy.

Alcindoro vainly tries to hush Musetta.

ALCINDORO: Quel canto scurrile mi muove la bile! Mi muove la bile!	That scurrilous song provokes my wrath! Provokes my wrath!
MUSETTA: E tu che sai, che memori e ti struggi, da me tanto rifuggi?	And you who know, who remember and are saddened, you turn from me thus?
MIMI: Io vedo ben che quella poveretta tutta invaghita ell'è!	*To Rodolfo.* I see very well that this poor girl is all in love!
MUSETTA: So ben: le angoscie tue non le vuoi dir, non le vuoi dir, so ben—ma ti senti morir!	I well know: you will not tell your anguish, you will not tell it, I well know, yet you feel yourself dying!
MIMI: —tutta invaghita di Marcel, tutta invaghita ell'è!	All in love with Marcel, she's all in love!

Schaunard and Colline get up and move to the side; they watch with great interest. Marcello rises to leave, but is rooted to the spot by Musetta's voice.

ALCINDORO: Quella gente, che dirà!	Those people, what will they say!
RODOLFO: Marcello un dì l'amò—	*To Mimi.* Once Marcello loved her—
SCHAUNARD: Ah! Marcello cederà!	Ah! Marcello is going to yield!
RODOLFO: —la fraschetta l'abbandonò—	—the flirt abandoned him—

Alcindoro vainly tries to make Musetta be still and eat.

COLLINE: Chi sa mai quel che avverrà!	Who knows what will ever happen!
RODOLFO: —per poi darsi a miglior vita—	—in order to lead a better life—
SCHAUNARD: Trovan dolce al pari il laccio—	One finds the snare as sweet as the other—
COLLINE: Santi numi, in simil briga—	Ye gods, in a like affair—
SCHAUNARD: —chi lo tende e chi ci dà!	—the one who sets it and the one who falls into it.
COLLINE: —mai Colline intopperà!	—Colline will never stumble into it!
MUSETTA: (Ah! Marcello smania—Marcello è vinto!)	(Ah! Marcello is raging—Marcello is conquered!)
ALCINDORO: Parla pian! Zitta, zitta!	Speak softly! Quiet, quiet!
MIMI: Quell'infelice mi muove a pietà!	I pity that unhappy girl!
COLLINE: Essa è bella, io non cieco—	She is beautiful, I'm not blind—

Mimi snuggles up to Rodolfo.

MIMI: T'amo!	I love you!

Rodolfo squeezes Mimi.

RODOLFO: Mimi!	Mimi!
SCHAUNARD: Quel bravaccio a momenti cederà! Stupenda è la commedia!	That bully is going to yield in a moment! The comedy is stupendous!

Musetta now faces Marcello.

MUSETTA: So bene angoscie tue non le vuoi dir. Ah! ma ti senti morir!	I well know your anguish, you will not tell it! Ah! Yet you feel yourself dying!

MIMI: Quell'infelice mi muove a pietà! L'amor ingeneroso è tristo amor! | I pity that unhappy girl! Ungenerous love is unhappy love!

RODOLFO: È fiacco amor quel che le offese vendicar non sa! Non risorge spento amor! | It's a feeble love that doesn't know how to avenge itself! A dead love doesn't revive!

COLLINE: —ma piaccion mi assai più una pipa e un testo greco, mi piaccion assai più! | —but a pipe and a Greek text please me much more, please me much more!

ALCINDORO: Modi, garbo! Zitta, zitta! | *Furiously.* Manners, nice manners! Quiet, quiet!

MUSETTA: Io voglio fare il mio piacere! Voglio far quel che mi par, non seccar! | I will do what I like! I will do whatever pleases me, don't bother me!

MIMI: Quell'infelice, ah! ah! mi muove, mi muove a pietà! | That unhappy girl, ah! ah! I pity, I pity her!

RODOLFO: È fiacco amore quel che le offese vendicar non sa! | It's a feeble love that doesn't know how to avenge itself!

SCHAUNARD: Se tal vaga persona ti trattasse a tu per tu, la tua scienza brontolona manderesti a Belzebù! | *To Colline.* If such an attractive person treated you to a tête-à-tête, you'd send your grumbling learning to the devil!

COLLINE: Essa è bella, non son cieco, ma—piaccion mi assai più una pipa e un testo greco! | She is beautiful, I'm not blind, but a pipe and a Greek text please me much more!

MUSETTA: (Ora convien liberarsi del vecchio!) | *Aside.* (Now is the time to get rid of the old man!)

She suddenly pretends to have such a pain in her foot that she must sit down again.

MUSETTA: Ahi! | Ow!

ALCINDORO: Che c'è?	What is it?
MUSETTA: Qual dolore, qual bruciore!	Such pain, such smarting!
ALCINDORO: Dove?	Where?
MUSETTA: Al piè!	In my foot!

Alcindoro indignantly unties Musetta's shoe.

MUSETTA: Sciogli, slaccia, rompi, straccia! te ne imploro—Laggiù c'è un calzolaio. Corri, presto!	Untie it, loosen it, break it, tear it! I beg you—Down there, there's a shoemaker. Run, quick!
MARCELLO: Gioventù mia—tu non sei morta—	My youth—you're not dead—
ALCINDORO: Imprudente!	Rash girl!
MUSETTA: Ne voglio un altro paio, ahi, che fitta, maledetta scarpa stretta.	I want another pair, ow, what a pain, damned tight shoe.

She puts the shoe on the table.

Or la levo—	Now I'll take it off——
MARCELLO: —nè di te morto è il sovvenir!	—nor is your memory dead!
ALCINDORO: Quella gente, che dirà?	Those people, what will they say?
SCHAUNARD & COLLINE: La commedia è stupenda—la commedia è stupenda!	The comedy is stupendous—the comedy is stupendous!
MARCELLO: Se tu battessi alla mia porta—t'andrebbe il mio core ad aprir, ad aprir!	If you knocked at my door, my heart would go to open, to open!
MUSETTA: Eccola qua. Corri, va, corri! Presto! Va! Va!	There it is, here. Run, go, run! Quick! Go! Go!
MIMI: Io vedo ben, ell'è invaghita di Marcello!	I well see, she's in love with Marcello!

(Courtesy Sadler's Wells Opera. Photo by Angus McBean)

Act. 2. The Bohemians at the Café Momus. A street vendor.

(Courtesy Royal Opera House, Covent Garden, London)

Act 2. Rodolfo and Mimi at the Café Momus, as portrayed by Rudolf Schock and Elisabeth Schwarzkopf.

Act 2, concluding scene, in an 1898 performance at the American Theater, New York.

RODOLFO: Io vedo ben—la commedia è stupenda!	I well see—the comedy is stupendous!

Alcindoro embarrassedly hides the shoe under his coat as he leaves.

ALCINDORO: Ma il mio grado! Vuoi ch'io comprometta? Aspetta! Musetta! Vo'!	But my dignity! Do you want me to be compromised? Wait! Musetta! I'm going!

As soon as Alcindoro is gone, Musetta and Marcello joyously fall into each others' arms.

MUSETTA: Marcello—	Marcello—
MARCELLO: Sirena—	Temptress—
SCHAUNARD: Siamo all'ultima scena!	We're at the final scene!

A waiter arrives with the bill.

RODOLFO, SCHAUNARD & COLLINE: Il conto?!	The bill?!
SCHAUNARD: Così presto?	So soon?
COLLINE: Chi l'ha richiesto?!	Who asked for it?!

The sounds of the parade are heard from the distance.

SCHAUNARD: Vediam!	Let's see!

Studies the bill and passes it around.

RODOLFO & COLLINE: Caro!	Expensive!
RODOLFO, SCHAUNARD & COLLINE: Fuori il danaro!	Out with the money!
SCHAUNARD: Colline, Rodolfo, e tu, Marcello?	Colline, Rodolfo, and you, Marcello?

Street arabs rush about excitedly.

STREET ARABS: La ritirata!	The changing of the guard!
MARCELLO: Siamo all'asciutto!	We're flat broke!
SCHAUNARD: Come?	What?

Workgirls, students, and citizens rush from Café.

WORKGIRLS, STUDENTS, CITIZENS: La ritirata! La ritirata!	The changing of the guard!

RODOLFO: Ho trenta soldi in tutto!
I have thirty cents in all!

People mill about, trying to determine from which direction the parade is coming.

MARCELLO, SCHAUNARD & COLLINE: Come? Non ce n'è più?
What? Isn't there any more?

SCHAUNARD: Ma il mio tesoro, ov'è!
But my treasure, where is it!

None of them find any money in their pockets, and they look at one another in great astonishment.

STREET ARABS: S'avvicinan per di qua!?
They'll come through this way!?

MUSETTA: Il mio conto date a me.
To the waiter. Give my bill to me.

WORKGIRLS & STUDENTS: No, di là!
No, from there!

STREET ARABS: S'avvicinan per di là!
They'll come through that way!

WORKGIRLS & STUDENTS: Vien di qua!
It's coming from here!

STREET ARABS: No, vien di là!
No, it's coming from there!

The waiter gives Musetta the bill.

MUSETTA: Bene!
Fine!

CITIZENS & HAWKERS: Largo! Largo!
Make way! Make way!

CHILDREN: Voglio veder! Voglio sentir!
I want to see! I want to hear!

MUSETTA: Presto, sommate quello con questo!
Quickly, add that to this!

CHILDREN: Mamma, voglio veder! Papà, voglio sentir!	Mama, I want to see! Papa, I want to hear!
MOTHERS: Lisetta, vuoi tacer! Tonio, vuoi finir!	Lisetta, will you be quiet! Tony, will you stop it!
MUSETTA: Paga il signor che stava qui con me!	The gentleman who was here with me will pay!
RODOLFO, MARCELLO, SCHAUNARD & COLLINE: Paga il signor!	The gentleman will pay!

They indicate where Alcindoro went out.

MOTHERS, ETC.: Vuò veder la ritirata!	He wants to see the changing of the guard!
OTHERS: Vuoi tacer, la vuoi finir?	Will you be quiet, will you stop it?
WORKGIRLS & STUDENTS: S'avvicinano di qua!	They'll come through this way!
WORKGIRLS, STUDENTS & HAWKERS: Sì, di qua!	Yes, this way.
STREET ARABS: Come sarà arrivata, la seguiremo al passo!	When it arrives, we'll follow it along the street!
COLLINE: Paga il signor!	*Amused and bemused.* The gentleman will pay!
SCHAUNARD: Paga il signor!	*With similar emotions.* The gentleman will pay!
MARCELLO: —il signor!	*With similar emotions.*—the gentleman!

Musetta takes both bills from the waiter and puts them at Alcindoro's place.

MUSETTA: E—dove s'è seduto, ritrovi il mio saluto.	And—may he find my greeting where he sits down!
HAWKERS: In quel rullio tu senti la patria maestà!	In that drum roll you hear the nation's majesty!

The sounds of the parade have been drawing nearer and nearer.

RODOLFO, MARCELLO, SCHAUNARD & COLLINE: E dove s'è seduto, ritrovi il suo saluto!	And may he find her greeting where he sits down!

As the parade approaches, the crowd makes way for it; the four friends and the girls remain in a group near the Café.

STREET ARABS: Ohè! Attenti, eccoli qua!	Oh! Look, there they are, here!
WORKGIRLS & STUDENTS: Largo, largo, eccoli qua!	Make way, make way, there they are, here!
MARCELLO: Giunge la ritirata!	The changing of the guard is arriving!
ENTIRE CROWD: —in fila!	—in a line!
MARCELLO & COLLINE: Che il vecchio non ci veda fuggir colla sua preda!	If only the old man doesn't see us fleeing with his prize!
RODOLFO: Giunge la ritirata!	The changing of the guard is arriving!
MARCELLO, SCHAUNARD & COLLINE: Quella folla serrata il nascondiglio appresti!	That dense crowd will supply us a hiding place!

The parade enters, led by a baton-twirling drum major.

ENTIRE CROWD: Ecco il tambur maggior! Più fier d'un antico guerrier!	There's the drum major! Fiercer than an ancient warrior!
PART OF CROWD: Il tambur maggior! Il tambur maggior!	The drum major! The drum major!
MIMI, MUSETTA, RODOLFO, SCHAUNARD & COLLINE: Lesti, lesti, lesti!	Quick, quick, quick!
CROWD: I Zappator, i Zappatori, olà! Ecco il tambur maggior!	The sappers, the sappers, hey there! There's the drum major!

WORKGIRLS: Il tambur maggior!	The drum major!
STUDENTS: Pare un general!	He looks like a general!
WORKGIRLS & STUDENTS: La ritirata è qua!	The changing of the guard is here!
BASSOS: Pare un general!	He looks like a general!
CROWD: Eccolo là! Il bel tambur maggior! La canna d'or, tutto splendor! Che guarda, passa, va!	There he is, there! The handsome drum major! The gold baton, all splendid! How he looks, walks, goes!
RODOLFO, MARCELLO, SCHAUNARD & COLLINE: Viva Musetta! Cuor birichin—	Long live Musetta! Artful heart—
CROWD: Tutta splendor! Di Francia è il più bell'uom!	All splendid! The handsomest man in France!
CROWD: Il bel tambur maggior! Eccolo là! Che guarda, passa, va!	The handsome drum major! There he is, there! How he looks, walks, goes!
RODOLFO, MARCELLO, SCHAUNARD & COLLINE: Gloria ed onor, onor e gloria del Quartier Latin!	Glory and honor, honor and glory of the Latin Quarter!

They follow the parade. Marcello and Colline triumphantly carry Musetta (who can't walk in only one shoe); Rodolfo and Mimi follow, arm in arm; Schaunard goes last, blowing his horn enthusiastically.

(Courtesy Gran Teatro del Liceo, Barcelona)

Setting for Act 3, with tollgate officials.

ACT THREE

(Courtesy Berlin Civic Opera. Photo by Scherl Studios)

Act 3. Mimi overhears as Rodolfo tells Marcello that she is mortally ill. Mimi is Maria Ivogün, Rodolfo is Koloman Pataky, and Marcello is Gerhard Huesch.

(Courtesy San Francisco Opera Association. Photo by Bill Cogan)

Act 3 quartet. As Marcello and Musetta revile each other, Rodolfo and Mimi agree to remain together until springtime. Left to right: Rolando Panerai as Marcello, Eugenia Ratti as Musetta, Lisa Della Casa as Mimi, and Gianni Raimondi as Rodolfo.

ACT THREE

Time: The following February.

Scene: Just outside one of the tollgates to Paris. A road leading off into the distance; an inn, with Marcello's painting, clearly labelled "At the Port of Marseilles," over the door; frescoes of a Turk and a Zouave on the inn walls. Gaunt, bare trees; everything is snow-covered. Laughter and the clinking of glasses come from inside the inn.

The curtain rises to a short, hollowly descriptive prelude. Street cleaners are approaching the tollgate, stamping their feet and blowing on their fingers because of the cold.

Street cleaners bang brooms and pails on the gate.

STREET CLEANERS: Ohè, là, le guardie. Aprite! Ohè, là! Quelli di Gentilly! Siam gli spazzini. Fiocca la neve—ohè, là—qui s'agghiaccia!

Ho, there, guards. Open up! Ho, there! Those from Gentilly! We're the sweepers. The snow is falling—ho, there—it's freezing here!

OFFICIAL: Vengo!

Sleepily. I'm coming.

Opens the gate, lets them through, and shuts it again. From inside the inn voices are heard, accompanied by clinking glasses.

VOICES: Chi nel ber trovò il piacer, nel suo bicchier, nel suo bicchier. Aa! d'una bocca nel ardor trovò l'amor, trovò l'amor!

Whoever found pleasure in drinking, in his glass, in his glass. Aa! From an ardent mouth found love, found love!

MUSETTA: Ah! Se nel bicchiere sta il piacer, in giovin bocca sta l'amor!

From inside. Ah! If pleasure is in the glass, love is a young mouth!

MEN: Tra le ral lè, tra le ral lè, Eva e Noè!

From inside. Tra le ral le, tra le ral le, Eve and Noah!

Milkwomen approach the tollgate.

MILKWOMEN: Houp-là! Houp-là!	Hoop-la! Hoop-la!
OFFICIAL: Son già le lattivendole.	It's already the milkwomen.

The gate is opened, the women go through; other peasant women, carters, etc. come along the road.

CARTERS: Houp-là!	Hoop-la!
PEASANT WOMEN: Houp-là!	Hoop-la!

Daylight breaks slowly as the various people are admitted through the gate.

SOME OF THE WOMEN: Buon giorno! Buon giorno! Buon giorno!	Good morning! Good morn-sing! Good morning!
OTHER WOMEN: Burro e cacio! Polli ed ova!	Butter and cheese! Chickens and eggs!
SOME WOMEN: Voi da che parte andate?	*To others.* Which way are you going?
OTHERS: A San Michele.	To Saint Michael's.
FIRST WOMEN: Ci troverem più tardi?	Shall we meet later?
OTHERS: A mezzodì!	At noon!
FIRST WOMEN: A mezzodì!	At noon!

They part in several different directions. Mimi comes out through the gate. She coughs badly, but finally manages to stop. Seeing the tollgate sergeant, she approaches him.

MIMI: Sa dirmi, scusi, qual'è l'osteria dove un pittor lavora?	Excuse me, can you tell me which is the inn where a painter is working?
SERGEANT: Eccola.	There it is.
MIMI: Grazie.	Thank you.

She goes up to a woman who has just come from the inn.

O buona donna, mi fate il favore di cercarmi il pittore Marcello? Ho da parlargli. Ho tanta fretta. Ditegli, piano, che Mimi l'aspetta.	Oh, good lady, do me the favor of looking up the painter Marcello for me? I have to speak to him. I'm in a great hurry. Tell him, softly, that Mimi is waiting for him.

The woman re-enters the inn. The customs official and his sergeant inspect other people as they come along the road.

SERGEANT: Ehi, quel paniere!	Hey, that basket!
OFFICIAL: Vuoto.	Empty.
SERGEANT: Passi.	You can go.

It is now bleak daylight. Various stragglers leave the inn. Matin sounds, and Marcello comes out.

MARCELLO: Mimi!	Mimi!
MIMI: Speravo di trovarvi qui.	I was hoping to find you here.
MARCELLO: È ver, siam qui da un mese; di quell'oste alle spese, Musetta insegna il canto ai passegieri—io pingo quei guerrieri sulla facciata.	It's true, we've been here for a month; for the expenses of mine host, Musetta teaches singing to travellers—I paint those warriors on the wall.

Indicates inn walls.

È freddo. Entrate.	It's cold. Come in.
MIMI: C'è Rodolfo?	Is Rodolfo there?
MARCELLO: Sì.	Yes.
MIMI: Non posso entrar, no, no!	I can't come in, no, no!
MARCELLO: Perchè?	Why?
MIMI: Oh! buon Marcello, aiuto! aiuto!	Oh! good Marcello, help! help!
MARCELLO: Cos'è avvenuto?	What has happened?
MIMI: Rodolfo, Rodolfo m'ama, Rodolfo m'ama e mi fugge, il mio Rodolfo si strugge per	Rodolfo, Rodolfo loves me, Rodolfo loves me, and flees from me. My Rodolfo is con-

gelosia. Un passo, un detto —un vezzo, un fior—lo mettono in sospetto. Onde corrucci ed ire. Talor la notte fingo di dormire e in me lo sento fiso spiarmi i sogni in viso. Mi grida ad ogni istante: non fai per me, ti prendi un altro amante, non fai per me! Ahimè! Ahimè! In lui parla il rovello, lo so, ma che rispondergli, Marcello?

sumed by jealousy. A step, a phrase—a glance, a flower—everything makes him suspicious. From there, worries and rages. Sometimes at night I pretend to sleep, and I feel him steadily reading the dreams in my face. Every moment he shouts at me: you're not for me, take yourself another lover, you're not for me! Alas! Alas! It's frenzy in him that speaks, I know that, but what shall I answer him, Marcello?

MARCELLO: Quando s'è come voi, non si vive in compagnia.

When it's as with you, one shouldn't live in company.

MIMI: Dite ben, dite bene. Lasciarci conviene. Aiutateci, aiutateci voi; noi s'è provato più volte, ma invano.

You're right, you're right. We ought to leave each other. Help us, help us; we've tried often, but in vain.

MARCELLO: Son lieve a Musetta, ell'è lieve a me, perchè ci amiamo in allegria—canti e risa, ecco il fior d'invariabile amor.

I'm lighthearted with Musetta, and she is lighthearted with me, because we love each other in gaiety—those are songs and laughter, that is the flower of a constant love.

MIMI: Dite ben—dite ben—lasciarci convien. Fate voi per il meglio.

You're right—you're right—we ought to leave each other. You arrange it for the best.

MARCELLO: Sta ben, sta ben. Ora lo sveglio.

Very well, very well. Now I'll wake him.

MIMI: Dorme?

Is he sleeping?

Marcello indicates that Mimi should look through the window.

MARCELLO: È piombato qui un'ora avanti l'alba, s'assopì sopra una panca, guardate.

He stumbled here an hour before dawn and fell asleep on a bench, look.

Mimi coughs violently.

Che tosse!

What a cough!

MIMI: Da ieri ho l'ossa rotte. Fuggì da me stanotte, dicendomi: È finita. A giorno sono uscita, e me ne venni a questa volta.

Coughing. It has racked my bones since yesterday. He fled from me tonight, saying: It's finished. At daybreak I went out and came here to this gate.

MARCELLO: Si desta—s'alza—mi cerca—viene—

He's waking—he's getting up—he's looking for me—he's coming—

MIMI: Ch'ei non mi veda!

He must not see me!

MARCELLO: Or rincasate. Mimi, per carità! Non fate scene qua!

Now go home. Mimi, for heaven's sake! Don't make a scene here!

Mimi conceals herself as Rodolfo hurries out of the inn to Marcello.

RODOLFO: Marcello. Finalmente! Qui niun ci sente, Io voglio separarmi da Mimi.

Marcello. At last! No one will hear us out here. I want to separate from Mimi.

MARCELLO: Sei volubil così?

Are you so inconstant?

RODOLFO: Già un'altra volta credetti morto il mio cor, ma di quegl'occhi azzurri allo splendor—esso è risorto. Ora il tedio l'assal—

Already once before, I thought my heart was dead, but at the splendor of those blue eyes, it was revived. Now weariness assails it—

MARCELLO: E gli vuoi rinnovare il funeral?

And you want to repeat the funeral for it?

RODOLFO: Per sempre!

Forever!

MARCELLO: Cambia metro.

Change your tune. It's the

Dei pazzi è l'amor tetro che lacrime distilla. Se non ride e sfavilla, l'amore è fiacco e roco. Tu sei geloso.

gloomy love of madmen that distills tears. If it doesn't laugh and sparkle, love grows weak and hoarse. You're jealous.

RODOLFO: Un poco.

A bit.

MARCELLO: Collerico, lunatico, imbevuto di pregiudizi, noioso, cocciuto.

Choleric, lunatic, full of prejudices, moody, headstrong.

MIMI: Or lo fa incollerir. Me poveretta!

Aside. Now he'll make him furious. Poor little me!

RODOLFO: Mimi è una civetta che frascheggia con tutti. Un moscardino di Viscontino le fa l'occhi di triglia. Ella sgonnella e scopre la caviglia con un far promettente e lusinghier—

Mimi is a coquette who flirts with everyone. A dandy of a little Viscount makes lovesick eyes at her. She flips up her skirts and displays her leg in a most promising and provocative way—

MARCELLO: Lo devo dir? Non mi sembri sincer.

Should I say it? You don't seem sincere to me.

RODOLFO: Ebbene, no, non lo son. Invan, invan nascondo —la mia vera tortura— Amo Mimi sovra ogni cosa al mondo io l'amo, ma ho paura, ma ho paura! Mimi è tanto malata! Ogni dì più declina. La povera piccina è condannata!

All right, then, no, I'm not. In vain, in vain I hide it, my real anguish—I love Mimi, I love her above everything in the world, but I'm afraid, I'm afraid! Mimi is so sick! Every day she gets worse. The poor little thing is doomed! . .

MARCELLO: Mimi?!

Mimi?

He tries to move Rodolfo out of Mimi's earshot.

MIMI: Che vuol dire?

What does he mean?

She moves closer to the others.

RODOLFO: Una terribile tosse l'esil petto le scuote, già le smunte gote di sangue rosse.

A terrible cough shakes her slender breast, yet her pale cheeks are flushed.

Marcello is upset, knowing that Mimi can hear. He tries to move Rodolfo further off.

MARCELLO: Povera Mimi!	Poor Mimi!
MIMI: Ahimè—morire!	*Weeping.* Alas—to die!
RODOLFO: La mia stanza è una tana squallida—il fuoco ho spento—v'entra e l'aggira il vento di tramontana. Essa canta e sorride, e il rimorso m'assale. Me cagion del fatale mal che l'uccide.	My room is a squalid hole—I've used up the fire—the north wind enters there and whirls around. She sings and smiles, and remorse attacks me. I am the cause of the fatal illness that's killing her.
MARCELLO: Che far dunque?	What to do, then?
MIMI: O mia vita!	O my life!
RODOLFO: Mimi di serra è fiore. Povertà l'ha sfiorita, per richiamarla in vita non basta amor, non basta amor.	Mimi is a hothouse flower. Poverty has withered her, love isn't enough to reclaim her to life, love isn't enough.
MIMI: Ahimè! Ahimè! È finita! O mia vita! È finita. Ahimè, morir, ahimè, morir!	Alas! Alas! It's finished. O my life! It's finished! Alas, to die, alas, to die!
MARCELLO: Oh qual pietà! Poveretta! Povera Mimi! Povera Mimi!	Oh such a pity! Poor little thing! Poor Mimi! Poor Mimi!

Mimi's coughing and sobbing give her away. Rodolfo runs to her.

RODOLFO: Ch'è? Mimi? Tu qui? M'hai sentito?	What's this? Mimi? You here? Did you hear me?
MARCELLO: Ella dunque ascoltava?!	Then she was listening?!

Rodolfo urges Mimi to enter the inn.

RODOLFO: Facile alla paura per nulla io m'arrovello. Vien là nel tepor.	I fly into a passion of fear far too easily over nothing. Come there, into the warmth.

MIMI: No, quel tanfo mi soffoca!	No, that moldy smell will stifle me!

Rodolfo embraces Mimi.

RODOLFO: Ah, Mimi!	Ah, Mimi!

Musetta's loud laugh is heard from the inn.

MARCELLO: È Musetta che ride. Con chi ride? Ah, la civetta? Imparerai!	It's Musetta who's laughing. With whom is she laughing? Ah, the flirt! You'll learn!

Rushes inside the inn.

MIMI: Addio.	Goodbye.

Frees herself from the embrace.

RODOLFO: Che! Vai?	What! You're going?
MIMI: Donde lieta uscì al tuo grido d'amore torna sola Mimi, al solitario nido. Ritorna un'altra volta a intesser finti fior! Addio senza rancor. Ascolta, ascolta. Le poche robe aduna che lasciai sparse. Nel mio cassetto stan chiusi quel cerchietto d'or, e il libro di preghiere. Involgi tutto quanto in un grembiale e manderò il portiere. Bada —sotto il guanciale c'è la cuffietta rosa. Se vuoi—se vuoi—se vuoi serbarla a ricordo d'amor! Addio, addio senza rancor!	Mimi returns alone to the solitary nest she gaily left at your call of love. She returns again to weave artificial flowers! Goodbye, without bitterness. Listen, listen. Collect the few scattered things that I left. In my drawer are locked that gold bracelet and the prayer book. Wrap them all up in an apron, and I'll send the porter. Look—under the pillow there's the pink bonnet. If you'd like—if you'd like—if you'd like to save it as a memento of love! Goodbye, goodbye without bitterness!
RODOLFO: Dunque è proprio finita! Te ne vai, te ne vai, la mia piccina. Addio, sogni d'amor!	Then it's really finished. You're going from here, you're going from here, my little one. Goodbye, dreams of love!
MIMI: Addio dolce svegliare alla mattina!	Goodbye sweet awakenings in the morning!

RODOLFO: Addio sognante vita—	Goodbye life of dreams—
MIMI: Addio rabuffi e gelosie!	*Gaily.* Goodbye rebuffs and jealousies!
RODOLFO: —Che un tuo sorriso acqueta!	—That one smile of yours could calm!
MIMI: Addio sospetti—	Goodbye doubts—
RODOLFO: Baci—	Kisses—
MIMI: —pungenti amarezze!	—poignant sorrows!
RODOLFO: —ch'io da vero poeta rimavo con carezze.	—that I, like a true poet, rhymed with caresses.
MIMI: Soli l'inverno è cosa da morire!	Solitude in winter is like dying!
RODOLFO: —Soli è cosa da morire!	Solitude is like dying!
MIMI: Soli!	Solitude!
MIMI & RODOLFO: Mentre a primavera c'è compagno il sol!	While in spring there's the sun for companion!
MIMI: C'è compagno il sol!	There's the sun for companion!

From the inn, the sound of breaking crockery..

MUSETTA: Che vuoi dir?	*From inside.* What do you mean?
MARCELLO: Che facevi? Che dicevi presso al fuoco a quel signore?	*From inside.* What were you doing? What were you saying to that gentleman near the fire?
MUSETTA: Che vuoi dir?	What do you mean?
MIMI: Niuno è solo l'april—	No one is alone in April—

She and Musetta meet at the inn door.

MARCELLO: Al mio venire hai mutato di colore.	At my coming you changed color.

He comes all the way outside.

MUSETTA: Quel signore mi diceva: ama il ballo, signorina?	*Defiantly.* That gentleman was saying to me: do you like dancing, miss?
RODOLFO: Si parla coi gigli e rose—	One can speak with the lilies and roses—
MARCELLO: Vana, frivola civetta!	Vain, frivolous flirt!
MUSETTA: Arrossendo rispondevo: ballerei sera e mattina, ballerei sera e mattina—	Blushing, I was answering: I could dance night and noon, I could dance night and noon—
MIMI: Esce dai nidi un cinguettio gentile—	A gentle chirping comes from the nests—
MARCELLO: Quel discorso asconde mire disoneste—	That conversation conceals dishonorable intentions—
MUSETTA: Voglio piena libertà!	I want complete freedom!
RODOLFO: Al fiorir di primavera—c'è compagno il sol!	At the blossoming of spring, there's the sun for companion!
MIMI: Al fiorir di primavera —c'è compagno il sol!	At the blossoming of spring, there's the sun for companion!
MARCELLO: —io t'acconcio per le feste se ti colgo a incivettire!	*Threateningly*—I'll thrash you if I catch you flirting!
MUSETTA: Che mi canti? Che mi gridi? Che mi canti? All'altar non siamo uniti!	What are you chanting at me? What are you shouting at me? What are you chanting at me? We haven't been united at the altar!
MARCELLO: Bada, sotto il mio cappello non ci stan certi ornamenti.*	Take care, there are not going to be certain ornaments under my cap.*

* This saying refers to the old belief that horns grew from a cuckold's head.

MUSETTA: Io detesto quegli amanti che la fanno da ah! ah! ah! ah! mariti!	I hate those lovers who act like ha! ha! ha! ha! husbands!
RODOLFO & MIMI: Chiacchieran le fontane—	The fountains chatter—
MARCELLO: Io non faccio da zimbello ai novizi intraprendenti.	I'm not going to be the laughing stock of your new conquests.
MIMI & RODOLFO: La brezza della sera—	The evening breeze—
MUSETTA: Fo' all'amor con chi mi piace!—non ti garba?	I'll make love with whomever I please!—doesn't that suit you?
MARCELLO: Vana, frivola civetta!	Vain, frivolous flirt!
MIMI & RODOLFO: —balsami stende—	—spreads balsam—
MUSETTA: —fo' all'amor con chi mi piace!	—I'll make love with whomever I please!
MARCELLO: Ve n'andate? Vi ringrazio: or son ricco divenuto. Vi saluto.	*With sarcasm.* You're going away? I thank you: now I've become rich. Good-bye.
MIMI & RODOLFO: —su le doglie umane—	—on human sorrows—
MUSETTA: Musetta se ne va—sì, se ne va! Vi saluto!	Musetta is leaving—yes, is leaving! Good-bye!
MIMI & RODOLFO: Vuoi che aspettiam la primavera ancor?	Do you still want us to wait for the spring?
MUSETTA: Signor, addio vi dico con piacer!	Sir, I bid you goodbye with pleasure!

Starts to stamp away in a fury.

MARCELLO: Son servo e me ne vo'!	Your servant, and goodbye!

Musetta turns and shouts.

MUSETTA: Pittore da bottega!	Shop painter!
MARCELLO: Vipera!	Viper!
MUSETTA: Rospo!	Lout!
MARCELLO: Strega!	Witch!

Stamps back into the inn.

MIMI: Sempre tua per la vita!	Always yours for life!

She and Rodolfo begin to move off, arm in arm.

RODOLFO: Ci lascieremo—	We'll leave each other—
MIMI: Ci lascieremo alla stagion dei fior!	We'll leave each other in the season of flowers!
RODOLFO: —alla stagion dei fior—	—in the season of flowers—
MIMI: Vorrei che eterno durasse il verno!	I wish that winter would last forever!

Their voices come from the distance.

MIMI & RODOLFO: Ci lascierem alla stagion dei fior!	We'll leave each other in the season of flowers!

ACT FOUR

(Courtesy Lyric Opera of Chicago. Photo by Nancy Sorensen)

Act 4. Rodolfo and Marcello reminisce about their lost loves. Richard Tucker as Rodolfo and Renato Cesari as Marcello in the 1960 production.

(Courtesy NBC Opera Company. NBC photo)

Act 4. Mimi's final illness. Left to right: Richard Torigi as Marcello, John Alexander as Rodolfo, Jan McArt as Musetta, and Dorothy Coulter as Mimi.

ACT FOUR

Time: Several months later.
Scene: Same as in Act I. MARCELLO is at his easel, trying to paint; RODOLFO pretends to be engrossed in writing. They are talking as the curtain goes up.

MARCELLO: In un coupè?	In a coupe?
RODOLFO: Con pariglia e livree. Mi salutò ridendo. To, Musetta! le dissi: e il cuor? "Non batte, o non lo sento, grazie al velluto che il copre."	With a team and livery. She hailed me, smiling. Hi, Musetta! I said to her: and your heart? "It's not beating, or I don't feel it, thanks to the velvet that covers it."
MARCELLO: Ci ho gusto davver, ci ho gusto davver!	*Pretending pleasure.* I'm really pleased about it, I'm really pleased about it!

Rodolfo resumes his writing.

RODOLFO: (Loiola va. Ti rodi e ridi.)	*Aside.* (That's rubbish. You're fretting, and you smile.)

Marcello energetically resumes painting.

MARCELLO: Non batte? Bene!— Io pur vidi—	Not beating? Good!— I also saw—
RODOLFO: —Musetta?	—Musetta?
MARCELLO: Mimi.	Mimi.

Rodolfo looks up excitedly before recovering his aplomb.

RODOLFO: L'hai vista? Oh guarda!	You've seen her? Oh really!

MARCELLO: Era in carrozza vestita come una regina.	She was in a carriage, dressed like a queen.
RODOLFO: Evviva. Ne son contento.	Well, grand. I'm glad of it.
MARCELLO: (Bugiardo, si strugge d'amor.)	*Aside.* (The liar, he's being consumed by love.)
RODOLFO: Lavoriam.	Let's work.
MARCELLO: Lavoriam.	Let's work.
RODOLFO: Che penna infame!	What an infamous pen!

Flings it away.

MARCELLO: Che infame pennello!	What an infamous paint brush!

Tosses it down. Rodolfo stares into space. Marcello furtively takes a bunch of ribbons from his pocket and kisses them.

RODOLFO: O Mimi, tu più non torni. O giorni belli, piccole mani, odorosi capelli—	O Mimi, you won't come back any more. O beautiful days, little hands, fragrant hair—

Marcello puts ribbons back into his pocket and also stares into space.

MARCELLO: Io non so come sia che il mio pennello lavori e impasti colori contro voglia mia.	I don't know how it is that my paint brush works and spreads colors against my wish.
RODOLFO: —collo di neve! Ah, Mimi, mia breve gioventù!	—snow white neck! Ah, Mimi, my brief youth!
MARCELLO: Se pingere mi piace o cieli o terre o inverni o primavere, egli mi traccia due pupille nere e una bocca procace, e n'esce di Musetta il viso ancor.	Whether I want to paint either skies or lands, either winters or springtides, it sketches two black eyes and a pert mouth, and out comes the face of Musetta again.

Rodolfo slyly takes Mimì's bonnet from the table-drawer and stares at it.

RODOLFO: E—tu, cuffietta lieve, che sotto il guancial partendo ascose, tutta sai la nostra felicità, vien sul mio cuor, sul mio cuor, sul mio cuor morto, ah, vien ah, vien, sul mio cuor; poichè è morto amor—	And you, light bonnet, that she, parting, hid under the pillow, you know all our happiness, come upon my heart, upon my heart, upon my dead heart, ah, come, ah, come upon my heart; since love is dead—
MARCELLO: —e n'esce di Musetta il viso tutto vezzi e tutto frode. Musetta intanto gode e il mio cuor vile la chiama, la chiama, e aspetta il vil mio cuor—	—and out comes the face of Musetta, all charms, all deception. Meanwhile, Musetta makes merry, and my base heart calls her, calls her, and my base heart waits.

Rodolfo holds bonnet to heart; then, dissembling . . .

RODOLFO: Che ora sia?	What time might it be?
MARCELLO: L'ora del pranzo di ieri.	Time for yesterday's dinner.
RODOLFO: E Schaunard non torna?	And Schaunard hasn't returned?

Enter Schaunard carrying four rolls, and Colline proudly bearing a herring in a bag.

SCHAUNARD: Eccoci!	Here we are!
RODOLFO: Ebben?	Well?

Schaunard and Colline put the food on the table.

MARCELLO: Ebben? Del pan?	Well? Some bread?
COLLINE: È un piatto degno di Demostene: un'aringa.	It's a dish worthy of Demosthenes: a herring.
SCHAUNARD: Salata.	Salted.
COLLINE: Il pranzo è in tavola.	Dinner is on the table.

All seat themselves with enormous dignity and pretend to be at a huge banquet.

MARCELLO: Questa è cuccagna da Berlingaccio.	This is a feast of plenty like Shrove Tuesday.

Schaunard places Colline's hat on the table and puts the water bottle inside it.

SCHAUNARD: Or lo sciampagna mettiamo in ghiaccio.	Now let's put the champagne on ice.

Rodolfo offers a roll to Marcello.

RODOLFO: Scelga, o Barone, trota o salmone?	Will you select, O Baron, trout or salmon?

Marcello accepts and gracefully turns to Schaunard.

MARCELLO: Duca, una lingua di pappagallo?	Duke, a parrot's tongue?

Schaunard refuses politely, pours a glass of water, and gives it to Marcello.

SCHAUNARD: Grazie, m'impingua. Stasera ho un ballo.	Thank you, it will make me fat. I have a dance tonight.

The glass is handed around. Colline hungrily eats his roll and gets up.

RODOLFO: Già sazio?	Already full?
COLLINE: Ho fretta. Il Re m'aspetta.	*Pompously.* I'm in a hurry. The King awaits me.
MARCELLO: C'è qualche trama?	Is there some plot?
RODOLFO: Qualche mister?	Some mystery?

Schaunard cocks his head inquisitively at Colline.

SCHAUNARD: Qualche mister?	Some mystery?
MARCELLO: Qualche mister?	Some mystery?

Colline strides back and forth importantly.

COLLINE: Il Re mi chiama al minister.	The King summons me to the ministry.
SCHAUNARD: Bene!	Good!
MARCELLO: Bene!	Good!
RODOLFO: Bene!	Good!

COLLINE: Però vedrò—vedrò —Guizot!*	*Patronizingly.* Thereupon I shall see—I shall see—Guizot!*
SCHAUNARD: Porgimi il nappo.	Hand me the cup.

Marcello gives him the glass.

MARCELLO: Sì! Bevi, io pappo!	Yes! You drink, I'm getting bloated!

Schaunard climbs on a chair and raises the glass.

SCHAUNARD: Mi sia permesso al nobile consesso—	May it be permitted to me by this noble assembly—
RODOLFO & COLLINE: Basta!	*Yelling.* Enough!
COLLINE: Che decotto! Dammi il gotto!	What a decoction! Give me the glass!
MARCELLO: Fiacco! Leva il tacco!	Destroy him! Push him down!

Schaunard signals for silence.

SCHAUNARD: M'ispira irresistibile l'estro della romanza—	The poetic rage of song inspires me irresistibly—
RODOLFO: No!!!	*Shouting.* No!!!
MARCELLO: No!!!	*Shouting.* No!!!
COLLINE: No!!!	*Shouting.* No!!!

With a martyred air, Schaunard resigns himself.

SCHAUNARD: Azione coreografica allora?	Choreographic action, then?
RODOLFO, MARCELLO & COLLINE: Sì, Sì!	Yes, yes!

All three applaud and pull Schaunard off the chair.

SCHAUNARD: La danza con musica vocale!	A dance with vocal music!

* French historian and politician. At the time this scene takes place, he was a member of the Chamber of Deputies.

COLLINE: Si sgombrino le sale!	The premises should be cleared!

They move the furniture out of the way.

COLLINE: Gavotta.	Gavotte.
MARCELLO: Minuetto.	Minuet.
RODOLFO: Pavanella.	Pavane.

Schaunard demonstrates a step.

SCHAUNARD: Fandango.	Fandango.
COLLINE: Propongo la quadriglia.	I propose the quadrille.

The others show enthusiastic approval.

RODOLFO: Mano alle dame!	Hands to the ladies!
COLLINE: Io detto.	I'll direct.

Schaunard importantly beats the time.

SCHAUNARD: Lallera, lallera, lallera, là. Lallera, lallera, lallera, là.	Lallera, lallera, lallera, la, Lallera, lallera, lallera, la.

Rodolfo bows very low to Marcello.

RODOLFO: Vezzosa damigella—	Charming damsel—

Marcello replies in a squeaky falsetto.

MARCELLO: Rispetti la modestia,—	Respect my modesty,—

In normal voice.

—la prego.	—I pray you.

Rodolfo and Marcello dance a quadrille.

SCHAUNARD: Lallera, lallera, lallera, là.	Lallera, lallera, lallera, la.
COLLINE: *Balancez!*	*Balancez!*
MARCELLO: Lallera, lallera, lallera.	Lallera, lallera, lallera.
SCHAUNARD: Prima c'è il *Rond.*	First there's the *Rond.*

COLLINE: No, bestia! | No, blockhead!

Rodolfo and Marcello continue dancing; Schaunard is exaggeratedly disdainful.

SCHAUNARD: Che modi da lacchè! | Manners like a lackey!

COLLINE: Se non erro, lei m'oltraggia! | *Haughtily.* If I am not mistaken, you have outraged me!

Seizes a poker from the fireplace.

Snudi il ferro! | Unsheath your sword!

Schaunard grabs the tongs.

SCHAUNARD: Pronti. Assaggia. Il tuo sangue io voglio ber. | Ready. Take this. I will drink your blood.

Rodolfo and Marcello watch and applaud heartily

COLLINE: Un di noi qui si sbudella. | One of us here will be disemboweled.

SCHAUNARD: Apprestate una barella. | Prepare a stretcher.

COLLINE: Apprestate un cimiter. | Prepare a graveyard.

They duel fiercely.

RODOLFO & MARCELLO: Mentre incalza la tenzone, gira e balza Rigodone.* | Whilst the combat rages, our rigadoon* leaps and turns.

Rodolfo and Marcello continue to dance; the duel grows more heated. The door bursts open and Musetta enters, greatly upset.

MARCELLO: Musetta! | Musetta!

MUSETTA: C'è Mimi—C'è Mimi, che mi segue e che sta male. | There's Mimi—There's Mimi who is following me and who is sick.

RODOLFO: Ov'è? Ah! | Where is she? Ah!

* *Rigadoon:* According to *Webster's Collegiate Dictionary*, this is a "lively dance with a jumping step for one couple."

Runs out to Mimi; Marcello follows. Schaunard and Colline drag forward the bed.

MUSETTA: Nel far le scale più non si resse.	She just couldn't do the stairs any more.
SCHAUNARD: Noi accostiamo quel lettuccio.	We'll drag up this old bed.

Rodolfo and Marcello help Mimi to the bed; Musetta gives her some water.

RODOLFO: Là. Da bere.	There. Something to drink.
MIMI: Rodolfo!	Rodolfo!
RODOLFO: Zitta, riposa.	Quiet, rest.

Mimi embraces Rodolfo.

MIMI: O mio Rodolfo! Mi vuoi qui con te?	Oh my Rodolfo! Do you want me here with you?
RODOLFO: Ah! mia Mimi, sempre, sempre!	Ah! Mimi, always, always!

Musetta and the others stand aside.

MUSETTA: Intesi dire che Mimi, fuggita dal Viscontino, era in fin di vita. Dove stia? Cerca, cerca—la veggo passar per via—trascinandosi a stento. Mi dice: "Più non reggo—muoio, lo sento. Voglio morir con lui! Forse m'aspetta."	I heard it said that Mimi, having fled from the little viscount, was at the end of her life. Where could she be? Search, search—I saw her going through the streets, dragging herself, with difficulty. She said to me: "I can't last much longer—I'm dying, I feel it. I want to die near him. Perhaps he's waiting for me."

Rodolfo has been helping to make Mimi comfortable; she stretches out full length on the bed.

MARCELLO: Sst!	*To Musetta.* Sst.
MIMI: Mi sento assai meglio—	I feel much better—

MUSETTA: "M'accompagni, Musetta?"	*In a softer tone.* "Would you come with me, Musetta?"
MIMI: —lascia ch'io guardi intorno. Ah, come si sta bene qui. Si rinasce, si rinasce—	—let me look around. Ah, it's so good to be here. Like being reborn, like being reborn—

Smiles contentedly.

RODOLFO: Benedetta bocca—	Most blessed mouth—
MIMI: Ancor—sento la vita qui—	Once more—I feel life here—
MUSETTA: Che ci avete in casa?	*To the others.* What have you in the house?
MARCELLO: Nulla.	Nothing.
MIMI: No . . . tu non mi lasci più!	No . . . you won't leave me any more!
RODOLFO: Tu ancor mi parli!	You're speaking to me again!
COLLINE: Nulla.	Nothing.
MUSETTA: Non caffè? Non vino?	No coffee? No wine?
MARCELLO: Nulla! Ah! miseria!	Nothing! Ah! poverty!

Schaunard sadly looks over at Mimi.

SCHAUNARD: Fra mezz'ora è morta.	In half an hour she'll be dead.
MIMI: Ho tanto freddo—se avessi un manicotto! Queste mie mani riscaldare non si potranno mai?	I'm so cold—if I just had a muff! Can't these hands ever be warm again?

Rodolfo chafes Mimi's hands in his.

RODOLFO: Qui, nelle mie! Taci! il parlar ti stanca.	Here, in mine! You should be still! Talking tires you.

Mimi greets the others as they come to her side.

MIMI: Ho un po' di tosse! Ci son avvezza. Buon giorno,	I have a slight cough! I'm used to it. Good day, Mar-

Marcello, Schaunard, Colline, buon giorno. Tutti qui, tutti qui—sorridenti a Mimi.	cello, Schaunard, Colline, good day. All here, all here—smiling at Mimi.
RODOLFO: Non parlar, non parlar.	Don't speak, don't speak.
MIMI: Parlo pian. Non temere.	I'll speak softly. Don't worry.

Motions to Marcello.

Marcello, date retta: è assai buona, Musetta.	Marcello, listen: Musetta is very good.
MARCELLO: Lo so—lo so.	I know it—I know it.

Schaunard and Colline remain aside. Schaunard sits with his face buried in his hands; Colline stares sadly into space. Musetta pulls Marcello aside, takes off her earrings and gives them to him.

MUSETTA: A te—vendi, riporta qualche cordial—manda un dottore!	For you—sell them, bring back some medicine—send a doctor!

Rodolfo pulls a chair beside the bed and sits down.

RODOLFO: Riposa.	Rest.
MIMI: Tu non mi lasci?	*Drowsily.* You won't leave me?
RODOLFO: No! No!	No! No!

Musetta draws aside Marcello as he is on his way out.

MUSETTA: Ascolta! Forse è l'ultima volta che ha espresso un desiderio, poveretta! Pel manicotto io vo'. Con te verrò.	Listen. Maybe it's the last time she has expressed a wish, poor little thing! I'll go for the muff. I'll come with you.
MARCELLO: Sei buona, o mia Musetta!	You're good, oh my Musetta!

Marcello and Musetta leave together. Colline takes off his coat and addresses it.

COLLINE: Vecchia zimarra, senti, io resto al pian, tu	Old gown, listen, I stay on the ground, now you must ascend

ascendere il sacro monte or devi—Le mie grazie ricevi. Mai non curvasti il logoro dorso ai ricchi ed ai potenti. Passar nelle tue tasche come in antri tranquilli filosofi e poeti. Ora che i giorni lieti fuggir, ti dico addio, fedele amico mio—addio, addio.	the sacred mount.* Receive my thanks. You never bent your threadbare back to the rich and to the powerful. Through your pockets, as through tranquil grottoes, passed philosophers and poets. Now that these happy days are gone, I bid you farewell, my faithful friend, farewell, farewell.

He folds the coat under his arm and starts to go; but seeing Schaunard, goes to him and pats his shoulder.

COLLINE: Schaunard, ognuno per diversa via, mettiamo insieme due atti di pietà; io—questo!—	Schaunard, each in his different way, together let's perform two acts of mercy; I—this!—

Indicates the coat.

E tu—lasciali soli là!	And you—leave them alone there!
SCHAUNARD: Filosofo, ragioni! È ver! Vo' via!	Philosopher, you're right! It's true! I'll go away!

Schaunard glances around. As an excuse for his leaving, he picks up the water bottle, and follows Colline out, softly shutting the door. Mimi opens her eyes and holds out her hands to Rodolfo.

MIMI: Sono andati? Fingevo di dormire—perchè volli con te sola restare. Ho tante cose che ti voglio dire—o una sola, ma grande come il mare—come il mare profonda ed infinita—Sei il mio amor—e tutta la mia vita. Sei il mio amore e tutta la mia vita.	Are they gone? I was pretending to sleep—because I wanted to stay alone with you. I have so many things I want to tell you—or only one thing, but as wide as the ocean—deep and infinite as the ocean—You're my love and all my life. You're my love and all my life.

* The pawn shop.

RODOLFO: Ah! Mimi, mia bella Mimi!	Ah! Mimi, my lovely Mimi!
MIMI: Son bella ancora?	Am I still lovely?
RODOLFO: Bella come un' aurora—	Lovely as a sunrise—
MIMI: Hai sbagliato il raffronto. Volevi dir—bella come un tramonto. "Mi chiamano Mimi—mi chiamano Mimi—il perchè non so—"	Your comparison is wrong. You meant—lovely as a sunset. "They call me Mimi—they call me Mimi—I don't know the reason—"

Rodolfo tenderly fetches the bonnet and gives it to her.

RODOLFO: Tornò al nido la rondine e cinguetta.	The swallow has come back to its nest and sings.

Helps Mimi put on the bonnet. She leans against him.

MIMI: La mia cuffietta, la mia cuffietta! Ah! Te lo rammenti quando sono entrata la prima volta, là?	My bonnet, my bonnet! Ah! Do you remember when I came in for the first time, there?
RODOLFO: Se lo rammento!	Do I remember!
MIMI: Il lume s'era spento—	The candle had gone out—
RODOLFO: Eri tanto turbata! Poi smarristi la chiave—	You were so upset! Then you lost the key—
MIMI: E a cercarla tastoni ti sei messo.	And you set yourself groping around to look for it.
RODOLFO: E cerca, cerca—	And looked, looked—
MIMI: Mio bel signorino, posso ben dirlo adesso lei la trovò—assai presto—	My fine little sir, I can tell you now, you found it quickly enough—
RODOLFO: Aiutavo il destino—	I was assisting fate—
MIMI: Era buio e il mio rossor non si vedeva—"Che gelida	It was dark, and my blushing couldn't be seen—"What a

manina, se la lasci riscaldar!" Era buio e la man tu mi prendevi.	frozen little hand, if you'd let it be warmed up!" It was dark, and you held my hand—

She has a sudden, violent coughing spell and sinks back, exhausted.

RODOLFO: Oh! Dio! Mimi!	Oh! Lord! Mimi!

Schaunard returns; seeing Rodolfo's distress, he rushes to the bedside.

SCHAUNARD: Che avvien?	What's happening?
MIMI: Nulla. Sto bene.	Nothing. I'm all right.
RODOLFO: Zitta, per carità.	Quiet, for pity's sake.
MIMI: Sì, sì, perdona. Or sarò buona.	Yes, yes, pardon me. Now I'll be good.

Musetta with a muff, and Marcello with medicine tiptoe in.

MUSETTA: Dorme?	*To Rodolfo.* Is she sleeping?
RODOLFO: Riposa.	She's resting.
MARCELLO: Ho veduto il dottore! Verrà; gli ho fatto fretta. Ecco il cordial.	I have seen the doctor! He will come; I asked him to hurry. Here is the medicine.

He finds a spirit lamp, sets it on the table, and lights it.

MIMI: Chi parla?	Who is speaking?

Musetta gives Mimi the muff.

MUSETTA: Io—Musetta—	I—Musetta—

Mimi seizes the muff with childish glee.

MIMI: O come è bello e morbido. Non più, non più le mani allividite. Il tepore le abbellirà.	Oh how soft and lovely it is. No more, no more will my hands grow pale with the cold. The warmth will keep them pretty.

To Rodolfo.

Sei tu che me lo doni?	Is it you who gives me this?
MUSETTA: Sì.	Yes.

Rodolfo weeps.

MIMI: Tu! Spensierato! Grazie! Ma costerà. Piangi? Sto bene— Pianger così, perchè? Qui amor— sempre con te! Le mani al caldo—e—dormire.

You! Spendthrift! Thank you! But what it must have cost! You cry? I am well— Why cry like that? Here, love—always with you. My hands in the warmth—and— to sleep.

Puts her hands in the muff and nods drowsily.
Rodolfo motions to the others to be still and addresses Marcello.

RODOLFO: Che ha detto il medico?

What did the doctor say?

MARCELLO: Verrà.

He will come.

Musetta heats the medicine over the spirit lamp. She prays almost without realizing it.

MUSETTA: Madonna benedetta, fate la grazia a questa poveretta che non debba morire. Qui ci vuole un riparo perchè la fiamma sventola.

Blessed Madonna, show grace to this poor little girl, that she need not die. This needs a screen here, because the flame flickers.

Motions to Marcello to shield the lamp-flame with a book.

Così. E che possa guarire. Madonna santa, io sono indegna di perdono, mentre invece Mimi è un angelo del cielo.

So. And that she will be able to get well. Holy Madonna, I am unworthy of pardon, while instead, Mimi is an angel of the heavens.

Rodolfo returns from the bedside.

RODOLFO: Io spero ancora. Vi pare che sia grave?

I am still hoping. Does it seem serious to you?

MUSETTA: Non credo.

I don't think so.

Schaunard tiptoes to the bedside. Horrified, he goes over to Marcello.

SCHAUNARD: Marcello, è spirata—

Marcello, she's dead—

A ray of light falls through the window onto Mimi. Musetta motions toward her cloak, which Rodolfo takes and tries to stretch across the window. Colline enters softly and lays some money on the table.

COLLINE: Musetta—a voi.	Musetta—for you.

He goes to help Rodolfo with the cloak.

Come va?	How is she?

Musetta signals to Rodolfo that the medicine is ready.

RODOLFO: Vedi? È tranquilla.	See? she's peaceful.

Notices the strange behavior of Marcello and Schaunard.

Che vuol dire quell'andare e venire—quel guardarmi così?	What does it mean, that coming and going—that looking at me this way?

Marcello goes to Rodolfo and puts an arm around his shoulder.

MARCELLO: Coraggio—	Courage—

Rodolfo rushes to the bedside. First he tries to rouse Mimi; then he falls across the bed, sobbing.

RODOLFO: Mimi! Mimi!	Mimi! Mimi!

The curtain goes down as the others stand in various attitudes of stunned grief. The original directions called for Marcello to turn his back to the footlights and sob, but this is not always carried out.

BIBLIOGRAPHY and CRITICAL COMMENTS

SOURCE OF ITALIAN LIBRETTO:

La Bohème. An Opera in Four Acts. Music by Giacomo Puccini, libretto by Giuseppe Giacosa and Luigi Illica. Arranged by Carlo Carignani. Vocal Score. G. Ricordi & Co., New York, 1896 and 1917.

REFERENCES:

Adami, Giuseppe (ed.). *Letters of Giacomo Puccini*. London, 1931. Letters written by Puccini from his student days to his death. Unfortunately, the editor, a close friend and admirer of the composer, has excluded material that shows Puccini in anything but a flattering light.

Carmer, Mosco. *Puccini, A Critical Biography*. New York: Alfred A. Knopf, 1959. The latest and best book on Puccini in English. Detailed and thoughtful critical study is given to each opera.

Del Fiorentino, Dante. *Immortal Bohemian: An Intimate Memoir of Giacomo Puccini*. New York, 1952. Informal glimpses of the composer at his Torre del Lago home.

Grout, Donald Jay. *A Short History of Opera*. New York: Columbia University Press, 1947. 2 volumes. A thorough study of opera from its beginnings to the present, including illustrations of changes in musical styles.

Krehbiel, Henry Edward. *More Chapters of Opera*. New York, 1919. Mostly history of opera productions in New York of the early 1900's, interwoven with critical comment.

Marek, George R. *Puccini: A Biography*. New York: Simon and Schuster, 1951. A first-rate job of biography, entertaining as well as informative.

——— *A Front Seat at the Opera.* New York, 1946. Critical, historical, and anecdotal background of operas, their composers, and the people who performed them. Includes what is probably some of the most amusing material ever compiled on the subject.

Martens, Frederick H. *A Thousand and One Nights of Opera.* New York, 1926. Plot summaries of operas, including lesser-known works based on the same sources as famous ones.

Melitz, Leo. *The Opera Goer's Complete Guide.* New York, 1911. Plot summaries—not altogether accurate, but what is lacking in quality is present in quantity.

Murger, Henri. *Bohemians of the Latin Quarter* (*Scènes de la vie de Bohème*). New York, 1912. Translation of the Murger work. The anonymous translator has done an excellent job, as has an anonymous introduction-writer.

Newman, Ernest. *Stories of the Great Operas and Their Composers.* New York: Alfred A. Knopf. A good, and, on the whole, accurate work.

Specht, Richard. *Giacomo Puccini: The Man, His Life, His Work.* New York, 1933. More of a remembrance and an appreciation than a biography. Contains some insights into the composer's personality and working habits.

CHRONOLOGICAL LIST OF PUCCINI'S WORKS

1. *Le Villi*—May 31, 1884.
2. *Edgar*—April 21, 1889.
3. *Manon Lescaut*—February 1, 1893.
4. *La Bohème*—February 1, 1896.
5. *Tosca*—January 14, 1900.
6. *Madama Butterfly*—February 17, 1904.
7. *La Fanciulla del West* ("The Girl of the Golden West")—December 10, 1910.
8. *La Rondine*—March 27, 1917.
9. *Il Trittico* ("The Triptych"):
   Il Tabarro, *Suor Angelica*, *Gianni Schicchi* — December 14, 1918
10. *Turandot*—April 25, 1926 (posthumous).

CATALOG OF DOVER BOOKS

Classics of Science

***OPTICKS, Sir Isaac Newton.** An enormous storehouse of insights and discoveries on light, reflection, color, refraction, theories of wave and corpuscular propagation of light, optical apparatus, and mathematical devices which have recently been reevaluated in terms of modern physics and placed in the top-most ranks of Newton's work. Foreword by Albert Einstein. Preface by I. B. Cohen of Harvard U. 7 pages of portraits, facsimile pages, letters, etc. cxvi + 412pp. 5⅜ x 8. S205 Paperbound **$2.00**

A SURVEY OF PHYSICAL THEORY, M. Planck. Lucid essays on modern physics for the general reader by the Nobel laureate and creator of the quantum revolution. Planck explains how the new concepts came into being; explores the clash between theories of mechanics, electrodynamics, and thermodynamics; and traces the evolution of the concept of light through Newton, Huygens, Maxwell, and his own quantum theory, providing unparalleled insights into his development of this momentous modern concept. Bibliography. Index. vii + 121pp. 5⅜ x 8. T650 Paperbound **$1.15**

DE RE METALLICA, Georgius Agricola. Written over 400 years ago, for 200 years the most authoritative first-hand account of the production of metals, translated in 1912 by former President Herbert Hoover and his wife, and today still one of the most beautiful and fascinating volumes ever produced in the history of science! 12 books, exhaustively annotated, give a wonderfully lucid and vivid picture of the history of mining, selection of sites, types of deposits, excavating pits, sinking shafts, ventilating, pumps, crushing machinery, assaying, smelting, refining metals, making salt, alum, nitre, glass, and many other topics. This definitive edition contains all 289 of the 16th century woodcuts which made the original an artistic masterpiece. It makes a superb gift for geologists, engineers, libraries, artists, historians, and everyone interested in science and early illustrative art. Biographical, historical introductions. Bibliography, survey of ancient authors. Indices. 289 illustrations. 672pp. 6¾ x 10¾. Deluxe library edition. S6 Clothbound **$10.00**

CHARLES BABBAGE AND HIS CALCULATING ENGINES, edited by P. Morrison and E. Morrison. Friend of Darwin, Humboldt, and Laplace, Babbage was a leading pioneer in large-scale mathematical machines and a prophetic herald of modern operational research—true father of Harvard's relay computer Mark I. His Difference Engine and Analytical Engine were the first successful machines in the field. This volume contains a valuable introduction on his life and work; major excerpts from his fascinating autobiography, revealing his eccentric and unusual personality; and extensive selections from "Babbage's Calculating Engines," a compilation of hard-to-find journal articles, both by Babbage and by such eminent contributors as the Countess of Lovelace, L. F. Menabrea, and Dionysius Lardner. 11 illustrations. Appendix of miscellaneous papers. Index. Bibliography. xxxviii + 3 pp. 5⅜ x 8. T12 Paperbound **$2.00**

A SOURCE BOOK IN MATHEMATICS, D. E. Smith. English translations of the original papers that announced the great discoveries in mathematics from the Renaissance to the end of the 19th century: succinct selections from 125 different treatises and articles, most of them unavailable elsewhere in English—Newton, Leibniz, Pascal, Riemann, Bernoulli, etc. 24 articles trace developments in the field of number, 18 cover algebra, 36 are on geometry, and 13 on calculus. Biographical-historical introductions to each article. Two volume set. Index in each. Total of 115 illustrations. Total of xxviii + 742pp. 5⅜ x 8. T552 Vol I Paperbound **$1.85**
T553 Vol II Paperbound **$1.85**
The set, boxed **$3.50**

***THE WORKS OF ARCHIMEDES WITH THE METHOD OF ARCHIMEDES, edited by T. L. Heath.** All the known works of the greatest mathematician of antiquity including the recently discovered METHOD OF ARCHIMEDES. This last is the only work we have which shows exactly how early mathematicians discovered their proofs before setting them down in their final perfection. A 186 page study by the eminent scholar Heath discusses Archimedes and the history of Greek mathematics. Bibliography. 563pp. 5⅜ x 8. S9 Paperbound **$2.00**

***THE THIRTEEN BOOKS OF EUCLID'S ELEMENTS, edited by T. L. Heath.** This is the complete EUCLID — the definitive edition of one of the greatest classics of the western world. Complete English translation of the Heiberg text with spurious Book XIV. Detailed 150 page introduction discusses aspects of Greek and medieval mathematics: Euclid, texts, commentators, etc. Paralleling the text is an elaborate critical exposition analyzing each definition, proposition, postulate, etc., and covering textual matters, mathematical analyses, refutations, extensions, etc. Unabridged reproduction of the Cambridge 2nd edition. 3 volumes. Total of 995 figures, 1426pp. 5⅜ x 8. S88, 89, 90 — 3 vol. set, Paperbound **$6.00**

CLASSICS OF CARDIOLOGY, F. A. Willius, T. E. Keys. Monumental collection of 52 papers by great researchers, physicians on the anatomy, physiology and pathology of the heart and the circulation, and the diagnosis and therapy of their diseases. These are the original writings of Harvey, Sénac, Auenbrugger, Withering, Stokes, Einthoven, Osler, and 44 others from 1628 to 1912. 27 of the papers are complete, the rest in major excerpts; all are in English. The biographical notes and introductory essays make this a full history of cardiology—with exclusively first-hand material. 103 portraits, diagrams, and facsimiles of title pages. Chronological table. Total of xx + 858pp. 5⅝ x 8⅜. Two volume set. S912 Vol I Paperbound **$2.00**
S913 Vol II Paperbound **$2.00**
The set **$4.00**

***A PHILOSOPHICAL ESSAY ON PROBABILITIES, P. Laplace.** Without recource to any mathematics above grammar school, Laplace develops a philosophically, mathematically and historically classical exposition of the nature of probability: its functions and limitations, operations in practical affairs, calculations in games of chance, insurance, government, astronomy, and countless other fields. New introduction by E. T. Bell. viii + 196pp. S166 Paperbound **$1.35**

***DIALOGUES CONCERNING TWO NEW SCIENCES, Galileo Galilei.** A classic of experimental science which has had a profound and enduring influence on the entire history of mechanics and engineering. Galileo based this, his finest work, on 30 years of experimentation. It offers a fascinating and vivid exposition of dynamics, elasticity, sound, ballistics, strength of materials, and the scientific method. Translated by H. Crew and A. de Salvio. 126 diagrams. Index. xxi + 288pp. 5⅜ x 8. S99 Paperbound **$1.65**

DE MAGNETE, William Gilbert. This classic work on magnetism founded a new science. Gilbert was the first to use the word "electricity," to recognize mass as distinct from weight, to discover the effect of heat on magnetic bodies; invented an electroscope, differentiated between static electricity and magnetism, conceived of the earth as a magnet. Written by the first great experimental scientist, this lively work is valuable not only as an historical landmark, but as the delightfully easy to follow record of a perpetually searching, ingenious mind. Translated by P. F. Mottelay. 25 page biographical memoir. 90 fix. lix + 368pp. 5⅜ x 8. S470 Paperbound **$2.00**

***THE GEOMETRY OF RENÉ DESCARTES.** The great work which founded analytic geometry. The renowned Smith-Latham translation faced with the original French text containing all of Descartes' own diagrams! Contains: Problems the Construction of Which Requires Only Straight Lines and Circles; On the Nature of Curved Lines; On the Construction of Solid or Supersolid Problems. Notes. Diagrams. 258pp. S68 Paperbound **$1.50**

Nature and Biology

THE AUTOBIOGRAPHY OF CHARLES DARWIN AND SELECTED LETTERS, edited by Francis Darwin. The personal record of the professional and private life of the author of "Origin of the Species," whose ideas have shaped our thinking as have few others. His early life; the historic voyage aboard the "Beagle," the furor surrounding evolution and his replies; revealing anecdotes; reminiscences by his son; letters to Henslow, Lyell, Hooker, Huxley, Wallace, Kingsley, and others; his thought on religion and vivisection. Appendix. Index. 365pp. 5⅜ x 8. T479 Paperbound **$1.65**

THE LIFE OF PASTEUR, R. Vallery-Radot. 13th edition of this definitive biography, cited in Encyclopaedia Britannica. Authoritative, scholarly, well-documented with contemporary quotes, observations; gives complete picture of Pasteur's personal life; especially thorough presentation of scientific activities with silkworms, fermentation, hydrophobia, inoculation, etc. Introduction by Sir William Osler. Index. 505pp. 5⅜ x 8. T632 Paperbound **$2.00**

LOUIS PASTEUR, S. J. Holmes. A brief, very clear, and warmly understanding biography of the great French scientist by a former Professor of Zoology in the University of California. Traces his home life, the fortunate effects of his education, his early researches and first theses, and his constant struggle with superstition and institutionalism in his work on microorganisms, fermentation, anthrax, rabies, etc. New preface by the author. T197 Paperbound **$1.00**

THE ORIGIN OF LIFE, A. I. Oparin. This is the first modern statement of the theory that life evolved from complex nitro-carbon compounds. A historical introduction covers theories of the origin of life from the Greeks to modern times and then the techniques of biochemistry as applied to the problem by Dr. Oparin. The exposition presupposes a knowledge of chemistry but can be read with profit by everyone interested in this absorbing question. "Easily the most scholarly authority on the question," NEW YORK TIMES. Bibliography. Index. xxv + 270pp. 5⅜ x 8. S213 Paperbound **$1.75**

FREE! All you do is ask for it!

A WAY OF LIFE, by Sir William Osler. An inspirational classic that has helped countless business and professional men since the beloved physician and philosopher first delivered it at Yale in 1913. In warm human terms Osler tells how he managed to make the most of every day by an edifying mental and physical regimen. Illustrated. **FREE**

STUDIES ON THE STRUCTURE AND DEVELOPMENT OF VERTEBRATES, Edwin S. Goodrich. This definitive study by the greatest modern comparative anatomist covers the skeleton, fins and limbs, head region morphology, skull, skeletal viseral arches and labial cartilages, middle ear and ear ossicles, visceral clefts and gills, subdivisions of body cavity, vascular, respiratory, excretory, and peripheral nervous systems of vertebrates from fish to the higher mammals. 754 pictures. 69 page biographical study by C. C. Hardy. Bibliography of 1186 references. "For many a day this will certainly be the standard textbook," Journal of Anatomy. Index. Two volumes total 906pp. 5⅜ x 8. 2 volume set S449-50 Paperbound **$5.00**

Music

A GENERAL HISTORY OF MUSIC, Charles Burney. A detailed coverage of music from the Greeks up to 1789, with full information on all types of music: sacred and secular, vocal and instrumental, operatic and symphonic. Theory, notation, forms, instruments, innovators, composers, performers, typical and important works, and much more in an easy, entertaining style. Burney covered much of Europe and spoke with hundreds of authorities and composers so that this work is more than a compilation of records . . . it is a living work of careful and first-hand scholarship. Its account of thoroughbass (18th century) Italian music is probably still the best introduction on the subject. A recent NEW YORK TIMES review said, "Surprisingly few of Burney's statements have been invalidated by modern research . . . still of great value." Edited and corrected by Frank Mercer. 35 figures. Indices. 1915pp. 5⅜ x 8. 2 volumes. T36 The Set, Clothbound **$12.50**

A DICTIONARY OF HYMNOLOGY, John Julian. This exhaustive and scholarly work has become known as an invaluable source of hundreds of thousands of important and often difficult to obtain facts on the history and use of hymns in the western world. Everyone interested in hymns will be fascinated by the accounts of famous hymns and hymn writers and amazed by the amount of practical information he will find. More than 30,000 entries on individual hymns, giving authorship, date and circumstances of composition, publication, textual variations, translations, denominational and ritual usage, etc. Biographies of more than 9,000 hymn writers, and essays on important topics such as Christmas carols and children's hymns, and many other unusual and valuable information. A 200 page double-columned index of first lines — the largest in print. Total of 1786 pages in two reinforced clothbound volumes. 6¼ x 9¼. The set, T333 Clothbound **$15.00**

MUSIC IN MEDIEVAL BRITAIN, F. Ll. Harrison. The most thorough, up-to-date, and accurate treatment of the subject ever published, beautifully illustrated. Complete account of institutions and choirs; carols, masses, and motets; liturgy and plainsong; and polyphonic music from the Norman Conquest to the Reformation. Discusses the various schools of music and their reciprocal influences; the origin and development of new ritual forms; development and use of instruments; and new evidence on many problems of the period. Reproductions of scores, over 200 excerpts from medieval melodies. Rules of harmony and dissonance; influence of Continental styles; great composers (Dunstable, Cornysh, Fairfax, etc.); and much more. Register and index of more than 400 musicians. Index of titles. General Index. 225-item bibliography. 6 Appendices. xix + 491pp. 5⅝ x 8¾. T705 Clothbound **$10.00**

THE MUSIC OF SPAIN, Gilbert Chase. Only book in English to give concise, comprehensive account of Iberian music; new Chapter covers music since 1941. Victoria, Albéniz, Cabezón, Pedrell, Turina, hundreds of other composers; popular and folk music; the Gypsies; the guitar; dance, theatre, opera, with only extensive discussion in English of the Zarzuela; virtuosi such as Casals; much more. "Distinguished . . . readable," Saturday Review. 400-item bibliography. Index. 27 photos. 383pp. 5⅜ x 8. T549 Paperbound **$2.00**

STRUCTURAL HEARING: TONAL COHERENCE IN MUSIC, Felix Salzer. Written by a pupil of the late Heinrich Schenker, this is not only the most thorough exposition in English of the Schenker method but also extends the Schenker approach to include modern music, the middle ages, and renaissance music. It explores the phenomenon of tonal organization by means of a detailed analysis and discussion of more than 500 musical pieces. It casts new light for the reader acquainted with harmony upon the understanding of musical compositions, problems of musical coherence, and connection between theory and composition. "Has been the foundation on which all teaching in music theory has been based at this college," Leopold Mannes, President of The Mannes College of Music. 2 volumes. Total of 658pp. 6½ x 9¼. The set, T418 Clothbound **$8.00**

ON STUDYING SINGING, Sergius Kagen. An intelligent method of voice-training, which leads you around pitfalls that waste your time, money, and effort. Exposes rigid, mechanical systems, baseless theories, deleterious exercises. "Logical, clear, convincing . . . dead right," Virgil Thomson, N.Y. Herald Tribune. "I recommend this volume highly," Maggie Teyte, Saturday Review. 119pp. 5⅜ x 8. T622 Paperbound **$1.25**

ROMAIN ROLLAND'S ESSAYS ON MUSIC, ed. by David Ewen. 16 best essays by great critic of our time, Nobel Laureate, discuss Mozart, Beethoven, Gluck, Handel, Berlioz, Wagner, Wolf, Saint-Saëns, Metastasio, Lully, Telemann, Grétry, "Origins of 18th Century 'Classic' Style," and musical life of 18th century Germany and Italy. "Shows the key to the high place that Rolland still holds in the world of music," Library Journal. 371pp. 5⅜ x 8. T550 Paperbound **$1.50**

WILLIAM LAWES, M. Lefkowitz. This is the definitive work on Lawes, the versatile, prolific, and highly original "King's musician" of 17th century England. His life is reconstructed from original documents, and nearly every piece he ever wrote is examined and evaluated: his fantasias, pavans, violin "sonatas," lyra viol and bass viol suites, and music for harp and theorbo; and his songs, masques, and theater music to words by Herrick ("Gather Ye Rose-buds"), Jonson, Suckling, Shirley, and others. The author shows the innovations of dissonance, augmented triad, and other Italian influences Lawes helped introduce to England. List of Lawes' complete works and several complete scores by this major precursor of Purcell and the 18th century developments. Index. 5 Appendices. 52 musical excerpts, many never before in print. Bibliography. x + 320pp. 5⅜ x 8. T706 Clothbound **$10.00**

JOHANN SEBASTIAN BACH, Philipp Spitta. The complete and unabridged text of the definitive study of Bach. Written some 70 years ago, it is still unsurpassed for its coverage of nearly all aspects of Bach's life and work. There could hardly be a finer non-technical introduction to Bach's music than the detailed, lucid analyses which Spitta provides for hundreds of individual pieces. 26 solid pages are devoted to the B minor mass, for example, and 30 pages to the glorious St. Matthew Passion. This monumental set also includes a major analysis of the music of the 18th century: Buxtehude, Pachelbel, etc. "Unchallenged as the last word on one of the supreme geniuses of music," John Barkham, SATURDAY REVIEW SYNDICATE. Total of 1819pp. 2 volumes. Heavy cloth binding. 5⅜ x 8. T252 Clothbound **$12.50**

THE LIFE OF MOZART, O. Jahn. Probably the largest amount of material on Mozart's life and works ever gathered together in one book! Its 1350 authoritative and readable pages cover every event in his life, and contain a full critique of almost every piece he ever wrote, including sketches and intimate works. There is a full historical-cultural background, and vast research into musical and literary history, sources of librettos, prior treatments of Don Juan legend, etc. This is the complete and unaltered text of the definitive Townsend translation, with foreword by Grove. 5 engraved portraits from Salzburg archives. 4 facsimiles in Mozart's hand. 226 musical examples. 4 Appendixes, including complete list of Mozart's compositions, with Köchel numbers (fragmentary works included). Total of xxviii + 1352pp. Three volume set, Bound in 2 volumes.

T85 Clothbound **$5.00**
T86 Clothbound **$5.00**
The set **$10.00**

THE FUGUE IN BEETHOVEN'S PIANO MUSIC, J. V. Cockshoot. The first study of a neglected aspect of Beethoven's genius: his ability as a writer of fugues. Analyses of early studies and published works demonstrate his original and powerful contributions to composition. 34 works are examined, with 143 musical excerpts. For all pianists, teachers, students, and music-minded readers with a serious interest in Beethoven. Index. 93-item bibliography. Illustration of original score for "Fugue in C." xv + 212pp. 5⅝ x 8⅜. T704 Clothbound **$6.00**

BEETHOVEN'S QUARTETS, J. de Marliave. The most complete and authoritative study ever written, enjoyable for scholar and layman alike. The 16 quartets and Grand Fugue are all analyzed bar by bar and theme by theme, not over-technically, but concentrating on mood and effects. Complete background material for each composition: influences, first reviews, etc. Preface by Gabriel Fauré. Introduction and notes by J. Escarra. Translated by Hilda Andrews. 321 musical examples. xxiii + 379pp. 5⅜ x 8.

T694 Paperbound **$1.85**